ND# MznLnx

Missing Links Exam Preps

Exam Prep for

Differential Geometry of Curves and Surfaces

DoCarmo, 1st Edition

The MznLnx Exam Prep is your link from the texbook and lecture to your exams.
The MznLnx Exam Preps are unauthorized and comprehensive reviews of your textbooks.

All material provided by MznLnx and Rico Publications (c) 2010
Textbook publishers and textbook authors do not particpate in or contribute to these reviews.

MznLnx

Rico
Publications

Exam Prep for Differential Geometry of Curves and Surfaces
1st Edition
DoCarmo

Publisher: Raymond Houge	*Product Manager:* Dave Mason
Assistant Editor: Michael Rouger	*Editorial Assitant:* Rachel Guzmanji
Text and Cover Designer: Lisa Buckner	*Pedagogy:* Debra Long
Marketing Manager: Sara Swagger	*Cover Image:* Jim Reed/Getty Images
Project Manager, Editorial Production: Jerry Emerson	*Text and Cover Printer:* City Printing, Inc.
Art Director: Vernon Lowerui	*Compositor:* Media Mix, Inc.

(c) 2010 Rico Publications

ALL RIGHTS RESERVED. No part of this work covered by the copyright may be reproduced or used in any form or by an means--graphic, electronic, or mechanical, including photocopying, recording, taping, Web distribution, information storage, and retrieval systems, or in any other manner--without the written permission of the publisher.

Printed in the United States
ISBN:

For more information about our products, contact us at:
Dave.Mason@RicoPublications.com

For permission to use material from this text or product, submit a request online to:
Dave.Mason@RicoPublications.com

Contents

CHAPTER 1
Curves   1

CHAPTER 2
Regular Surfaces   18

CHAPTER 3
The Geometry of the Gauss Map   39

CHAPTER 4
The Intrinsic Geometry of Surfaces   60

CHAPTER 5
Global Differential Geometry   87

ANSWER KEY   101

TO THE STUDENT

COMPREHENSIVE

The *MznLnx* Exam Prep series is designed to help you pass your exams. Editors at MznLnx review your textbooks and then prepare these practice exams to help you master the textbook material. Unlike study guides, workbooks, and practice tests provided by the texbook publisher and textbook authors, *MznLnx* gives you **all** of the material in each chapter in exam form, not just samples, so you can be sure to nail your exam.

MECHANICAL

The MznLnx Exam Prep series creates exams that will help you learn the subject matter as well as test you on your understanding. Each question is designed to help you master the concept. Just working through the exams, you gain an understanding of the subject--its a simple mechanical process that produces success.

INTEGRATED STUDY GUIDE AND REVIEW

MznLnx is not just a set of exams designed to test you, its also a comprehensive review of the subject content. Each exam question is also a review of the concept, making sure that you will get the answer correct without having to go to other sources of material. You learn as you go! Its the easiest way to pass an exam.

HUMOR

Studying can be tedious and dry. MznLnx's instructional design includes moderate humor within the exam questions on occassion, to break the tedium and revitalize the brain

Chapter 1. Curves

1. The _____, after the plane and the catenoid, is the third minimal surface to be known. It was first discovered by Jean Baptiste Meusnier in 1776. For every point on the _____ there is a helix contained in the _____ which passes through that point.

The _____ is shaped like Archimedes' screw, but extends infinitely in all directions. It can be described by the following parametric equations in Cartesian coordinates:

where $>\rho$ and $>\theta$ range from negative infinity to positive infinity, while $>\alpha$ is a constant. If $>\alpha$ is positive then the _____ is right-handed; if negative then left-handed.

   a. Scherk surface
   b. Weaire-Phelan structure
   c. Helicoid
   d. -module

2. _____s with given closed support are used in the construction of smooth partitions of unity ; these are essential in the study of smooth manifolds, for example to show that Riemannian metrics can be defined globally starting from their local existence. A simple case is that of a bump function on the real line, that is, a _____ f that takes the value 0 outside an interval [a,b] and such that

Given a number of overlapping intervals on the line, bump functions can be constructed on each of them, and on semi-infinite intervals (->∞, c] and [d,+>∞) to cover the whole line, such that the sum of the functions is always 1.

From what has just been said, partitions of unity don't apply to holomorphic functions; their different behavior relative to existence and analytic continuation is one of the roots of sheaf theory.

   a. 1-center problem
   b. Smooth function
   c. 11-cell
   d. -module

3. In geometry, the _____ line (or simply the _____) to a curve at a given point is the straight line that 'just touches' the curve at that point (in the sense explained more precisely below.) As it passes through the point of tangency, the _____ line is 'going in the same direction' as the curve, and in this sense it is the best straight-line approximation to the curve at that point. The same definition applies to space curves and curves in n-dimensional Euclidean space.
   a. Cartan connection
   b. Measuring function
   c. Metric signature
   d. Tangent

4. In mathematics, _____ refers to any of a number of loosely related concepts in different areas of geometry. Intuitively, _____ is the amount by which a geometric object deviates from being flat, or straight in the case of a line, but this is defined in different ways depending on the context. There is a key distinction between extrinsic _____, which is defined for objects embedded in another space (usually a Euclidean space) in a way that relates to the radius of _____ of circles that touch the object, and intrinsic _____, which is defined at each point in a differential manifold.
   a. Stiefel manifold
   b. Four-vertex theorem
   c. Curvature
   d. Second fundamental form

5. In mathematics, a _____ consists of the points through which a continuously moving point passes. This notion captures the intuitive idea of a geometrical one-dimensional object, which furthermore is connected in the sense of having no discontinuities or gaps. Simple examples include the sine wave as the basic _____ underlying simple harmonic motion, and the parabola.
   a. Singular point
   b. Sectrix of Maclaurin
   c. Dual curve
   d. Curve

6. A _____ is a visual representation of an area--a symbolic depiction highlighting relationships between elements of that space such as objects, regions, and themes.

Many _____s are static two-dimensional, geometrically accurate (or approximately accurate) representations of three-dimensional space, while others are dynamic or interactive, even three-dimensional. Although most commonly used to depict geography, _____s may represent any space, real or imagined, without regard to context or scale; e.g. Brain mapping, DNA mapping, and extraterrestrial mapping.

a. Map
b. -module
c. 11-cell
d. 1-center problem

7. A function or map from one topological space to another is called _____ if the inverse image of any open set is open. If the function maps the real numbers to the real numbers (both spaces with the Standard Topology), then this definition of _____ is equivalent to the definition of _____ in calculus. If a _____ function is one-to-one and onto and if the inverse of the function is also _____, then the function is called a homeomorphism and the domain of the function is said to be homeomorphic to the range.

   a. Metric space
   b. Continuous
   c. -module
   d. Fresnel integrals

8. In mathematics, the _____ is an operation which takes two vectors over the real numbers R and returns a real-valued scalar quantity. It is the standard inner product of the orthonormal Euclidean space. It contrasts with the cross product which produces a vector result.

The _____ of two vectors a = [a_1, a_2, …, a_n] and b = [b_1, b_2, …, b_n] is defined as:

where >Σ denotes summation notation and n is the dimension of the vectors.

   a. 1-center problem
   b. -module
   c. 11-cell
   d. Dot product

9. In linear algebra, functional analysis and related areas of mathematics, a _____ is a function that assigns a strictly positive length or size to all vectors in a vector space, other than the zero vector. A seminorm (or pseudonorm), on the other hand, is allowed to assign zero length to some non-zero vectors.

A simple example is the 2-dimensional Euclidean space R^2 equipped with the Euclidean _____.

a. Quasinorm
b. Bounded
c. Matrix norm
d. Norm

10. In mathematics, the _____ of a differentiable manifold M is the disjoint union of the tangent spaces of M. That is,

where T_xM denotes the tangent space to M at the point x. So an element of TM can be thought of as a pair (x, v), where x is a point in M and v is a tangent vector to M at x. There is a natural projection

defined by >π(x, v) = x.

a. Regular homotopy
b. Cerf theory
c. Tangent bundle
d. Differential topology

11. In mathematics, a _____ is a generalization of a fiber _____ dropping the condition of a local product structure. The requirement of a local product structure rests on the _____ having a topology. Without this requirement, more general objects can be considered _____s.
a. 1-center problem
b. 11-cell
c. -module
d. Bundle

12. In geometry, an _____ is a closed segment of a differentiable curve in the two-dimensional plane; for example, a circular _____ is a segment of the circumference of a circle. If the _____ segment occupies a great circle (or great ellipse), it is considered a great-_____ segment.

The length of an _____ of a circle with radius r and subtending an angle > (measured in radians) with the circle center -- i.e., the central angle -- equals >.

Chapter 1. Curves 5

a. Equiangular polygon
b. Order-4 dodecahedral honeycomb
c. Almost symplectic manifold
d. Arc

13. For some curves there is a smallest number L that is an upper bound on the length of any polygonal approximation. If such a number exists, then the curve is said to be rectifiable and the curve is defined to have _____ L.

Let C be a curve in Euclidean (or, more generally, a metric) space $X = R^n$, so C is the image of a continuous function f : [a, b] >→ X of the interval [a, b] into X.

a. AA postulate
b. ADE classification
c. ADHM construction
d. Arc length

14. In mathematics, an _____ on a real vector space is a choice of which ordered bases are 'positively' oriented and which are 'negatively' oriented. In the three-dimensional Euclidean space, the two possible basis _____s are called right-handed and left-handed (or right-chiral and left-chiral), respectively. However, the choice of _____ is independent of the handedness or chirality of the bases (although right-handed bases are typically declared to be positively oriented, they may also be assigned a negative _____.)

a. Apex
b. Adams-hemisphere-in-a-square
c. Apollonius' theorem
d. Orientation

15. A _____ on a curve is one where it is not smooth, for example, at a cusp.

The precise definition of a _____ depends on the type of curve being studied.

Algebraic curves in R^2 are defined as the zero set $f^{-1}(0)$ for a polynomial function $f:R^2 \rightarrow R$.

a. Singular point
b. Bicorn
c. Sextic plane curve
d. Secant line

16. In geometry, topology and related branches of mathematics a spatial _____ describes a specific object within a given space that consists of neither volume, area, length, nor any other higher dimensional analogue. Thus, a _____ is a 0-dimensional object. Because of their nature as one of the simplest geometric concepts, they are often used in one form or another as the fundamental constituents of geometry, physics, vector graphics, and many other fields.

   a. -module
   b. Bounded
   c. 1-center problem
   d. Point

17. A _____ is a curve derived from a fixed point O and two other curves >α and >β. Every line through O cutting >α at A and >β at B cuts the _____ at the midpoint of >.

The simplest expression uses polar coordinates with O at the origin. If r = >α(>θ) and r = >β(>θ) express the two curves then > expresses the _____.

   a. Cissoid
   b. Whewell equation
   c. Trisectrix of Maclaurin
   d. Quadrifolium

18. A _____ is the curve defined by the path of a point on the edge of circular wheel as the wheel rolls along a straight line. It is an example of a roulette, a curve generated by a curve rolling on another curve.

The _____ is the solution to the brachistochrone problem (i.e. it is the curve of fastest descent under gravity) and the related tautochrone problem (i.e. the period of a ball rolling back and forth inside it does not depend on the ball's starting position).

   a. Hippopede
   b. Cycloid
   c. Secant line
   d. Vesica piscis

19. _____ is the curve along which a small object moves, under the influence of friction, when pulled on a horizontal plane by a piece of thread and a puller that moves at a right angle to the initial line between the object and the puller at an infinitesimal speed. It is therefore a curve of pursuit. It was first introduced by Claude Perrault in 1670, and later studied by Sir Isaac Newton and Christian Huygens (1692.)

a. Positively oriented curve
b. Tautochrone
c. Tractrix
d. Singular point

20. In geometry, the _____ is an algebraic curve defined by the equation

$$\,>.$$

It forms a loop in the first quadrant with a double point at the origin and asymptote

$$\,>.$$

It is symmetrical about y = x.

a. Secant line
b. Folium of Descartes
c. Deltoid
d. Parallel

21. A _____, equiangular spiral or growth spiral is a special kind of spiral curve which often appears in nature. The _____ was first described by Descartes and later extensively investigated by Jakob Bernoulli, who called it Spira mirabilis, 'the marvelous spiral'.

In polar coordinates (r,>θ) the curve can be written as

$$\,>$$

or

$$\,>$$

with e being the base of natural logarithms, and a and b being arbitrary positive real constants.

a. Cotes' spiral
b. Padovan cuboid spiral
c. Sacks spiral
d. Logarithmic spiral

22. In mathematics, a _____ is a curve which emanates from a central point, getting progressively farther away as it revolves around the point. An Archimedean _____, a helix, and a conic _____.

A '_____' and a 'helix' are two terms that are easily confused, but represent different objects.

A _____ is typically a planar curve (that is, flat), like the groove on a record or the arms of a _____ galaxy.

a. Spiral of Theodorus
b. Cotes' spiral
c. Logarithmic spiral
d. Spiral

23. In formal mathematical logic, the concept of a _____ may be taken to mean a formula that can be derived according to the derivation rules of a fixed formal system. The statements of a theory as expressed in a formal language are called its elementary _____s and are said to be true.

The essential property of _____s is that they are derivable using a fixed set of inference rules and axioms without any additional assumptions.

a. Logical axioms
b. Theorem
c. Rule of inference
d. Proof

24. In mathematics, the _____ is a binary operation on two vectors in a three-dimensional Euclidean space that results in another vector which is perpendicular to the plane containing the two input vectors. The algebra defined by the _____ is neither commutative nor associative. It contrasts with the dot product which produces a scalar result. The _____ is also useful as a measure of 'perpendicularness'--the magnitude of the _____ of two vectors is equal to the product of their magnitudes if they are perpendicular and scales down to zero when they are parallel. The _____ is also known as the vector product, or Gibbs vector product.

a. Cross product
b. -module
c. Commutative
d. Linear map

25. _____ is the boundless, three-dimensional extent in which objects and events occur and have relative position and direction. Physical _____ is often conceived in three linear dimensions, although modern physicists usually consider it, with time, to be part of the boundless four-dimensional continuum known as spacetime. In mathematics _____s with different numbers of dimensions and with different underlying structures can be examined.

a. -module
b. 11-cell
c. 1-center problem
d. Space

26. In Riemannian geometry, the _____ at p consist of a chart such that locally the symmetric part of the Christoffel symbols vanish, i.e. $\Gamma^a_{(bc)} = 0$. Furthermore, at p, the following equations hold

$$g_{ij}(p) = \delta_{ij}, \quad \frac{\partial g_{ij}}{\partial x^k}(p) = 0, \quad \Gamma^i_{jk}(p) = 0.$$

Therefore, the covariant derivative reduces to a partial derivative, and the geodesics through p are locally linear functions of t. This idea was implemented by Einstein in his General Relativity using his Equivalence Principle and understanding the _____ as an inertial frame.

a. Normal coordinates
b. Riemannian circle
c. Cotton tensor
d. Riemannian geometry

27. In differential geometry of curves, the _____ of a sufficiently smooth plane curve at a given point on the curve is the circle whose center lies on the inner normal line and whose curvature is the same as that of the given curve at that point. This circle, which is the one among all tangent circles at the given point that approaches the curve most tightly, was named circulum osculans by Leibniz.

The center and radius of the _____ at a given point are called center of curvature and radius of curvature of the curve at that point.

Chapter 1. Curves

   a. Incenter
   b. Incircle
   c. AA postulate
   d. Osculating circle

28. In mathematics, a _____ is a flat surface. _____s can arise as subspaces of some higher dimensional space, as with the walls of a room, or they may enjoy an independent existence in their own right, as in the setting of Euclidean geometry
   a. Simple polytope
   b. Pendent
   c. Plane
   d. Parallelogram law

29. A _____ is a simple shape of Euclidean geometry consisting of those points in a plane which are the same distance from a given point called the centre. The common distance of the points of a _____ from its center is called its radius.

_____s are simple closed curves which divide the plane into two regions, an interior and an exterior.

   a. Gergonne point
   b. Circumscribed circle
   c. Circumcircle
   d. Circle

30. A _____ is a number that determines the location of a point along some line or curve. A list of two, three, or more _____s can be used to determine the location of a point on a surface, volume, or higher-dimensional domain.

For example, the longitude is a _____ which determines the position of a point along the Earth's equator, and latitude is another _____ that defines a poisition along a meridian.

   a. 1-center problem
   b. 11-cell
   c. -module
   d. Coordinate

Chapter 1. Curves

31. In mathematics, particularly in differential geometry, an _____ is a plane in a Euclidean space or affine space which meets a submanifold at a point in such a way as to have a second order of contact at the point. The word osculate is from the Latin osculatus which is a past participle of osculari, meaning to kiss. An _____ is thus a plane which 'kisses' a submanifold.
    a. Osculating Plane
    b. Omnitruncated 5-cell
    c. Order-5 dodecahedral honeycomb
    d. Exterior bundle

32. In vector calculus, the _____ describe the kinematic properties of a particle which moves along a continuous, differentiable curve in three-dimensional Euclidean space R^3. More specifically, the formulas describe the derivatives of the so-called tangent, normal, and binormal unit vectors in terms of each other.
    a. Frenet-Serret formulas
    b. Fundamental theorem of curves
    c. Differential geometry of curves
    d. Classification of electromagnetic fields

33. In differential geometry, the two _____ at a given point of a surface measure how the surface bends by different amounts in different directions at that point.

At each point p of a differentiable surface in 3-dimensional Euclidean space one may choose a unit normal vector. A normal plane at p is one that contains the normal, and will therefore also contain a unique direction tangent to the surface and cut the surface in a plane curve.

    a. Gaussian curvature
    b. Menger curvature
    c. Geodesic curvature
    d. Principal curvatures

34. The distance from the center of a sphere or ellipsoid to its surface is its radius. The equivalent 'surface radius' that is described by radial distances at points along the body's surface is its _____ . With a sphere, the _____ equals the radius.
    a. Lie sphere geometry
    b. Radius of curvature
    c. Diffeology
    d. G_2 manifold

Chapter 1. Curves

35. In mathematics, a _____ is a curve in a Euclidian plane (cf. space curve.) The most frequently studied cases are smooth _____s (including piecewise smooth _____s), and algebraic _____s.
    a. Heilbronn triangle problem
    b. Point group in two dimensions
    c. Plane curve
    d. Chirality

36. In the elementary differential geometry of curves in three dimensions, the _____ of a curve measures how sharply it is twisting. Taken together, the curvature and the _____ of a space curve are analogous to the curvature of a plane curve. For example, they are coefficients in the system of differential equations for the Frenet frame given by the Frenet-Serret formulas.
    a. Symmetric space
    b. Torsion
    c. G-structure
    d. Darboux vector

37. In mathematics, a commutative ring R is _____ if for any pair of prime ideals

    p, q,

any two strictly increasing chains

   $p = p_0 \supset \subset p_1 ... \supset \subset p_n = q$ of prime ideals

are contained in maximal strictly increasing chains from p to q of the same (finite) length. In other words, there is a well-defined function from pairs of prime ideals to natural numbers, attaching to p and q the length of any such maximal chain.

   a. Catenary
   b. Cotangent complex
   c. Deformation theory
   d. Cone of curves

38. In the differential geometry of curves, the _____ of a curve is the locus of all its centers of curvature. Equivalently, it is the envelope of the normals to a curve. The original curve is an involute of its _____.

a. Induced metric
b. Evolute
c. Information geometry
d. Isothermal coordinates

39. In mathematics, two vectors are _____ if they are perpendicular, i.e., they form a right angle. The word comes from the Greek >á½€>ρ>θϊŒ>ς , meaning 'straight', and >>γ>ω>vῑ >α (gonia), meaning 'angle'. For example, a subway and the street above, although they do not physically intersect, are _____ if they cross at a right angle.
a. Interior algebra
b. Orthogonal
c. Algebraic K-theory
d. Embedding

40. In Euclidean geometry, a _____ is moving every point a constant distance in a specified direction. It is one of the rigid motions (other rigid motions include rotation and reflection.) A _____ can also be interpreted as the addition of a constant vector to every point, or as shifting the origin of the coordinate system.
a. Reflection
b. Point reflection
c. Rotation of axes
d. Translation

41. In mathematics, a _____ could be any function mapping a set X onto another set or onto itself. However, often the set X has some additional algebraic or geometric structure and the term '_____' refers to a function from X to itself which preserves this structure.

Examples include linear _____s and affine _____s such as rotations, reflections and translations.

a. Transformation
b. 1-center problem
c. -module
d. Codomain

42. In mathematics, the _____ system is a two-dimensional coordinate system in which each point on a plane is determined by a distance from a fixed point and an angle from a fixed direction.

The fixed point (analogous to the origin of a Cartesian system) is called the pole, and the ray from the pole with the fixed direction is the polar axis. The distance from the pole is called the radial coordinate or radius, and the angle is the angular coordinate, polar angle, or azimuth.

a. 1-center problem
b. -module
c. Polar coordinate
d. 11-cell

43. A _____ of a concept is an extension of the concept to less-specific criteria. It is a foundational element of logic and human reasoning. _____ posits the existence of a domain or set of elements, as well as one or more common characteristics shared by those elements.
   a. 11-cell
   b. 1-center problem
   c. -module
   d. Generalization

44. A curve $\boxed{\times}$ is said to be closed or a loop if $\boxed{\times}$ and if $\boxed{\times}$. A _____ is thus a continuous mapping of the circle S^1; a simple _____ is also called a Jordan curve or a Jordan arc. The Jordan curve theorem states that such curves divide the plane into an 'interior' and an 'exterior'.
   a. 1-center problem
   b. -module
   c. 11-cell
   d. Closed Curve

45. In mathematics, a _____ is a planar simple closed curve (that is, a curve in the plane whose starting point is also the end point and which has no other self-intersections) such that when traveling on it one always has the curve interior to the left (and consequently, the curve exterior to the right.) If in the above definition one interchanges left and right, one obtains a negatively oriented curve.

Crucial to this definition is the fact that every simple closed curve admits a well-defined interior; that follows from the Jordan curve theorem.

   a. Cissoid of Diocles
   b. Brachistochrone curve
   c. Trisectrix of Maclaurin
   d. Positively oriented curve

Chapter 1. Curves

46. The _____ is a geometric inequality involving the square of the circumference of a closed curve in the plane and the area of a plane region it encloses, as well as its various generalizations. Isoperimetric literally means 'having the same perimeter'. The isoperimetric problem is to determine a plane figure of the largest possible area whose boundary has a specified length.
    a. Inverse function theorem
    b. Isoperimetric inequality
    c. ADE classification
    d. AA postulate

47. In mathematics, an _____ is a statement about the relative size or order of two objects, or about whether they are the same or not

    - The notation a < b means that a is less than b.
    - The notation a > b means that a is greater than b.
    - The notation a ≠ b means that a is not equal to b, but does not say that one is bigger than the other or even that they can be compared in size.

    In all these cases, a is not equal to b, hence, '_____'.

    These relations are known as strict _____

    - The notation a ≤ b means that a is less than or equal to b (or, equivalently, not greater than b);
    - The notation a ≥ b means that a is greater than or equal to b (or, equivalently, not smaller than b);

    An additional use of the notation is to show that one quantity is much greater than another, normally by several orders of magnitude.

    - The notation a .

    a. ADE classification
    b. ADHM construction
    c. Inequality
    d. AA postulate

48. In geometry, a polygon can be either _____ or concave.

A _____ polygon is a simple polygon whose interior is a _____ set. The following properties of a simple polygon are all equivalent to convexity:

- Every internal angle is less than 180 degrees.
- Every line segment between two vertices remains inside or on the boundary of the polygon.

A simple polygon is strictly _____ if every internal angle is strictly less than 180 degrees. Equivalently, a polygon is strictly _____ if every line segment between two nonadjacent vertices of the polygon is strictly interior to the polygon except at its endpoints.

   a. Convex combination
   b. Supporting hyperplane
   c. Convex
   d. Separating axis theorem

49. A _____ is a movement of an object in a circular motion. A two-dimensional object rotates around a center (or point) of _____. A three-dimensional object rotates around a line called an axis.
   a. Curve of constant width
   b. Similarity
   c. Square lattice
   d. Rotation

50. In the geometry of curves a _____ is a point of where the first derivative of curvature is zero. This is typically a local maximum or minimum of curvature. Other special cases may occur, for instance when the second derivative is also zero, or when the curvature is constant.
   a. Coordinate-induced basis
   b. Non-Euclidean crystallographic group
   c. Holomorphic vector bundle
   d. Vertex

51. A _____ of a curve is the envelope of a family of congruent circles centered on the curve. It generalises the concept of _____ lines.

It is sometimes called the offset curve but the term 'offset' often refers also to translation.

a. Cissoid
b. Parallel
c. Trisectrix of Maclaurin
d. Cassini oval

52. In mathematics, the _____ or convex envelope for a set of points X in a real vector space V is the minimal convex set containing X.

In computational geometry, it is common to use the term '_____' for the boundary of the minimal convex set containing a given non-empty finite set of points in the plane. Unless the points are collinear, the _____ in this sense is a simple closed polygonal chain.

a. Geodesic convexity
b. Convex combination
c. Convex hull
d. Separating axis theorem

Chapter 2. Regular Surfaces

1. A _____ is a number that determines the location of a point along some line or curve. A list of two, three, or more _____s can be used to determine the location of a point on a surface, volume, or higher-dimensional domain.

   For example, the longitude is a _____ which determines the position of a point along the Earth's equator, and latitude is another _____ that defines a poisition along a meridian.

   a. Coordinate
   b. 11-cell
   c. 1-center problem
   d. -module

2. In mathematics and its applications, a _____ is a system for assigning an n-tuple of numbers or scalars to each point in an n-dimensional space. This concept is part of the theory of manifolds. 'Scalars' in many cases means real numbers, but, depending on context, can mean complex numbers or elements of some other commutative ring.
   a. -module
   b. 11-cell
   c. Coordinate system
   d. 1-center problem

3. In technical applications of 3D computer graphics (CAx) such as computer-aided design and computer-aided manufacturing, _____s are one way of representing objects. The other ways are wireframe (lines and curves) and solids. Point clouds are also sometimes used as temporary ways to represent an object, with the goal of using the points to create one or more of the three permanent representations.
   a. Solid modeling
   b. Space partitioning
   c. Geometric primitive
   d. Surface

4. In mathematics, a _____ consists of the points through which a continuously moving point passes. This notion captures the intuitive idea of a geometrical one-dimensional object, which furthermore is connected in the sense of having no discontinuities or gaps. Simple examples include the sine wave as the basic _____ underlying simple harmonic motion, and the parabola.
   a. Sectrix of Maclaurin
   b. Singular point
   c. Dual curve
   d. Curve

Chapter 2. Regular Surfaces   19

5. A function or map from one topological space to another is called _____ if the inverse image of any open set is open. If the function maps the real numbers to the real numbers (both spaces with the Standard Topology), then this definition of _____ is equivalent to the definition of _____ in calculus. If a _____ function is one-to-one and onto and if the inverse of the function is also _____, then the function is called a homeomorphism and the domain of the function is said to be homeomorphic to the range.

   a. Fresnel integrals
   b. -module
   c. Continuous
   d. Metric space

6. In Riemannian geometry, a _____ is a vector field along a geodesic >γ in a Riemannian manifold describing the difference between the geodesic and an 'infinitesimally close' geodesic. In other words, the _____s along a geodesic form the tangent space to the geodesic in the space of all geodesics. They are named after Carl Jacobi.

   a. Spin structure
   b. Weyl tensor
   c. Harmonic map
   d. Jacobi field

7. In every _____ there is a cuboid with all vertices tangent to the surface of said _____. It immediately becomes apparent that the cuboid inscribed in the _____ must be a cube with all vertices tangent to the surface of the _____.

Formula 1, shown below, finds the length of one side of the inscribed cube, and Formula 2 finds the volume of the inscribed cube.

   a. Sphere
   b. Cone
   c. Circumference
   d. Point group in two dimensions

8. In mathematics, a _____ is a point on the domain of a function where:

   - one dimension: the derivative (or slope of the line when visualized) is equal to zero or a point where the function ceases to be differentiable.
   - in general: there are two distinct concepts: either the derivative (Jacobian) vanishes, or it is not of full rank (or, in either case, the function is not differentiable); these agree in one dimension.

Note that in one dimension, a critical value or critical number x of function f is the domain element at which the derivative is zero or undefined, whereas the associated ordered pair (x, y) is the _____. In higher dimensions a critical value is in the range whereas a _____ is in the domain.

There are two situations in which a point becomes a _____ of a function of one variable. The first of which is that the value of the first derivative is equal to zero.

    a. Hessian matrix
    b. Monkey saddle
    c. Saddle surface
    d. Critical point

9. In differential topology, a _____ of a differentiable function between differentiable manifolds is the image of a critical point.

The basic result on _____s is Sard's lemma. The set of _____s can be quite irregular; but in Morse theory it becomes important to consider real-valued functions on a manifold M, such that the set of _____s is in fact finite.

    a. -module
    b. 1-center problem
    c. 11-cell
    d. Critical value

10. In geometry, topology and related branches of mathematics a spatial _____ describes a specific object within a given space that consists of neither volume, area, length, nor any other higher dimensional analogue. Thus, a _____ is a 0-dimensional object. Because of their nature as one of the simplest geometric concepts, they are often used in one form or another as the fundamental constituents of geometry, physics, vector graphics, and many other fields.
    a. -module
    b. Point
    c. Bounded
    d. 1-center problem

11. In mathematics, the image of a subset of the domain of a function under the function is the set of all possible outputs obtained when the function is evaluated at each element of the domain. The _____ or preimage of a particular subset of the codomain of a function is the set of all elements of the domain whose values under the function lie in the chosen subset of the codomain.

The word 'image' is used in three related ways.

a. ADE classification
b. AA postulate
c. ADHM construction
d. Inverse image

12. An _____ is a type of quadric surface that is a higher dimensional analogue of an ellipse. The equation of a standard axis-aligned _____ body in an xyz-Cartesian coordinate system is

where a and b are the equatorial radii (along the x and y axes) and c is the polar radius (along the z-axis), all of which are fixed positive real numbers determining the shape of the _____.

More generally, a not-necessarily-axis-aligned _____ is defined by the equation

where A is a symmetric positive definite matrix and x is a vector.

a. ADE classification
b. AA postulate
c. Ellipsoid
d. ADHM construction

13. In mathematics, a _____ is a quadric, a type of surface in three dimensions, described by the equation

_____ of one sheet,

or

_____ of two sheets.

These are also called elliptical _____s. If, and only if, a = b, it is a _____ of revolution, and is also called a circular _____.

a. 1-center problem
b. -module
c. 11-cell
d. Hyperboloid

14. In geometry, a _____ is a surface of revolution generated by revolving a circle in three dimensional space about an axis coplanar with the circle, which does not touch the circle. Examples of tori include the surfaces of doughnuts and inner tubes.
    a. Developable surface
    b. Gaussian surface
    c. PDE surfaces
    d. Torus

15. In differential geometry, the _____ of a point on a surface is the product of the principal curvatures, $>\kappa_1$ and $>\kappa_2$, of the given point. It is an intrinsic measure of curvature, i.e., its value depends only on how distances are measured on the surface, not on the way it is embedded in space. This result is the content of Gauss's Theorema egregium.

Symbolically, the _____ $>K$ is defined as

$$\boxed{} >.$$

where $>\kappa_1$ and $>\kappa_2$ are the principal curvatures.

    a. Menger curvature
    b. Geodesic curvature
    c. Principal curvatures
    d. Gaussian curvature

16. In mathematics, _____ refers to any of a number of loosely related concepts in different areas of geometry. Intuitively, _____ is the amount by which a geometric object deviates from being flat, or straight in the case of a line, but this is defined in different ways depending on the context. There is a key distinction between extrinsic _____, which is defined for objects embedded in another space (usually a Euclidean space) in a way that relates to the radius of _____ of circles that touch the object, and intrinsic _____, which is defined at each point in a differential manifold.
    a. Curvature
    b. Stiefel manifold
    c. Four-vertex theorem
    d. Second fundamental form

Chapter 2. Regular Surfaces

17. In linear algebra, a (linear) _____ is a subset of a vector space that is closed under multiplication by positive scalars. In other words, a subset C of a real vector space V is a _____ if and only if >λx belongs to C for any x in C and any positive scalar >λ of V (or, more succinctly, if and only if >λC = C for any positive scalar >λ.)

A _____ is said to be pointed if it includes the null vector (origin) 0; otherwise it is said to be blunt.

 a. Complex line
 b. Prismatic surface
 c. Centerpoint
 d. Cone

18. A _____ is one of the most curvilinear basic geometric shapes:It has two faces, zero vertices, and zero edges. The surface formed by the points at a fixed distance from a given straight line, the axis of the _____. The solid enclosed by this surface and by two planes perpendicular to the axis is also called a _____.
 a. -module
 b. Cylinder
 c. Bounded
 d. 1-center problem

19. In differential geometry, the _____ maps a surface in Euclidean space R^3 to the unit sphere S^2. Namely, given a surface X lying in R^3, the _____ is a continuous map N: X >→ S^2 such that N(p) is a unit vector orthogonal to X at p, namely the normal vector to X at p.

The _____ can be defined (globally) if and only if the surface is orientable, in which case its degree is half the Euler characteristic.

 a. Gauss-Codazzi equations
 b. Weingarten equations
 c. Ridge
 d. Gauss map

20. A _____ is a visual representation of an area--a symbolic depiction highlighting relationships between elements of that space such as objects, regions, and themes.

Many _____s are static two-dimensional, geometrically accurate (or approximately accurate) representations of three-dimensional space, while others are dynamic or interactive, even three-dimensional. Although most commonly used to depict geography, _____s may represent any space, real or imagined, without regard to context or scale; e.g. Brain mapping, DNA mapping, and extraterrestrial mapping.

24 Chapter 2. Regular Surfaces

   a. 11-cell
   b. Map
   c. 1-center problem
   d. -module

21. In geometry, the _____ is a particular mapping (function) that projects a sphere onto a plane. The projection is defined on the entire sphere, except at one point -- the projection point. Where it is defined, the mapping is smooth and bijective.
   a. Mercator projection
   b. Stereographic projection
   c. 1-center problem
   d. -module

22. In mathematical analysis, a _____ is a classification of functions according to the properties of their derivatives. Higher order _____es correspond to the existence of more derivatives. Functions that have derivatives of all orders are called smooth.
   a. Differentiability class
   b. 1-center problem
   c. 11-cell
   d. -module

23. In mathematics, a _____ is an isomorphism of smooth manifolds. It is an invertible function that maps one differentiable manifold to another, such that both the function and its inverse are smooth. The image of a rectangular grid on a square under a _____ from the square onto itself.

Given two manifolds M and N, a bijective map f from M to N is called a _____ if both

and its inverse

are differentiable (if these functions are r times continuously differentiable, f is called a C^r-_____.)

Chapter 2. Regular Surfaces

a. -module
b. 11-cell
c. 1-center problem
d. Diffeomorphism

24. A _____ is a movement of an object in a circular motion. A two-dimensional object rotates around a center (or point) of _____. A three-dimensional object rotates around a line called an axis.
   a. Square lattice
   b. Similarity
   c. Curve of constant width
   d. Rotation

25. _____ generally conveys two primary meanings. The first is an imprecise sense of harmonious or aesthetically-pleasing proportionality and balance; such that it reflects beauty or perfection. The second meaning is a precise and well-defined concept of balance or 'patterned self-similarity' that can be demonstrated or proved according to the rules of a formal system: by geometry, through physics or otherwise.
   a. Crystal system
   b. Tessellation
   c. Screw axis
   d. Symmetry

26. In the sky, a _____ is an imaginary great circle on the celestial sphere. It passes through the north point on the horizon, through the celestial pole, up to the zenith, through the south point on the horizon, and through the nadir, and is perpendicular to the local horizon.

Because it is fixed to the local horizon, stars will appear to drift past the local _____ as the earth spins.

   a. Spring Meridian
   b. Poles of astronomical bodies
   c. Right ascension
   d. Meridian

27. A _____ of a curve is the envelope of a family of congruent circles centered on the curve. It generalises the concept of _____ lines.

It is sometimes called the offset curve but the term 'offset' often refers also to translation.

a. Trisectrix of Maclaurin
b. Cassini oval
c. Cissoid
d. Parallel

28. In mathematics, a _____ is a generalization of the notion of a 'straight line' to 'curved spaces'. In the presence of a metric, _____s are defined to be (locally) the shortest path between points on the space. In the presence of an affine connection, _____s are defined to be curves whose tangent vectors remain parallel if they are transported along it.
   a. Gauge theory
   b. Volume
   c. Minkowski space
   d. Geodesic

29. A _____ is a surface created by rotating a curve lying on some plane (the generatrix) around a straight line (the axis of rotation) that lies on the same plane.

Examples of surfaces generated by a straight line are the cylindrical and conical surfaces. A circle that is rotated about a (coplanar) axis through the center generates a sphere.

   a. Definite integral
   b. -module
   c. 1-center problem
   d. Surface of revolution

30. The _____, are coordinate-space expressions for the Levi-Civita connection derived from the metric tensor. In broader sense, the connection coefficients of an arbitrary (not necessarily metric) affine connection in a coordinate basis are often called _____. The _____ may be used for performing practical calculations in differential geometry.

The _____ are defined by:

Definition

The _____ can be derived from the vanishing of the covariant derivative of the metric tensor:

As a shorthand notation, the nabla symbol and the partial derivative symbols are frequently dropped, and instead a semi-colon and a comma are used to set off the index that is being used for the derivative. Thus, the above is sometimes written as

a. Cartan-Karlhede algorithm
b. Hopf-Rinow theorem
c. Killing vector field
d. Christoffel symbols

31. A _____ on a curve is one where it is not smooth, for example, at a cusp.

The precise definition of a _____ depends on the type of curve being studied.

Algebraic curves in R^2 are defined as the zero set $f^{-1}(0)$ for a polynomial function $f:R^2 \to R$.

a. Sextic plane curve
b. Singular point
c. Bicorn
d. Secant line

32. In geometry, the _____ line (or simply the _____) to a curve at a given point is the straight line that 'just touches' the curve at that point (in the sense explained more precisely below.) As it passes through the point of tangency, the _____ line is 'going in the same direction' as the curve, and in this sense it is the best straight-line approximation to the curve at that point. The same definition applies to space curves and curves in n-dimensional Euclidean space.
a. Measuring function
b. Cartan connection
c. Metric signature
d. Tangent

Chapter 2. Regular Surfaces

33. The _____ A : $S^n \to S^n$, defined by A(x) = −x, sends every point on the sphere to its antipodal point. It is homotopic to the identity map if n is odd, and its degree is $(-1)^{n+1}$.

If one wants to consider antipodal points as identified, one passes to projective space

   a. Antipodal map
   b. ADE classification
   c. AA postulate
   d. ADHM construction

34. In mathematics, two vectors are _____ if they are perpendicular, i.e., they form a right angle. The word comes from the Greek ὀρθός, meaning 'straight', and γωνία (gonia), meaning 'angle'. For example, a subway and the street above, although they do not physically intersect, are _____ if they cross at a right angle.
   a. Algebraic K-theory
   b. Interior algebra
   c. Embedding
   d. Orthogonal

35. In mathematics, a _____ is a quadric surface of special kind. There are two kinds of _____s: elliptic and hyperbolic. The elliptic _____ is shaped like an oval cup and can have a maximum or minimum point.
   a. Steiner surfaces
   b. PDE surfaces
   c. Parametric surface
   d. Paraboloid

36. With a = b an elliptic paraboloid is a _____: a surface obtained by revolving a parabola around its axis. It is the shape of the parabolic reflectors used in mirrors, antenna dishes, and the like; and is also the shape of the surface of a rotating liquid, a principle used in liquid mirror telescopes. It is also called a circular paraboloid.
   a. 11-cell
   b. 1-center problem
   c. -module
   d. Paraboloid of revolution

37. In mathematics, a _____ is a flat surface. _____s can arise as subspaces of some higher dimensional space, as with the walls of a room, or they may enjoy an independent existence in their own right, as in the setting of Euclidean geometry

a. Simple polytope
b. Parallelogram law
c. Pendent
d. Plane

38. In mathematics, more specifically differential topology, a _____ is intuitively a function between smooth manifolds that preserves the local differentiable structure. The formal definition of a _____ is given below.
    a. Reeb foliation
    b. Toroid
    c. Donaldson theory
    d. Local Diffeomorphism

39. In geometry and trigonometry, an _____ is the figure formed by two rays sharing a common endpoint, called the vertex of the _____ . The magnitude of the _____ is the 'amount of rotation' that separates the two rays, and can be measured by considering the length of circular arc swept out when one ray is rotated about the vertex to coincide with the other Where there is no possibility of confusion, the term '_____' is used interchangeably for both the geometric configuration itself and for its angular magnitude (which is simply a numerical quantity.)
    a. ADE classification
    b. AA postulate
    c. Angle
    d. ADHM construction

40. In Riemannian geometry, the _____ at p consist of a chart such that locally the symmetric part of the Christoffel symbols vanish, i.e. $\Gamma^a_{(bc)} = 0$. Furthermore, at p, the following equations hold

$$g_{ij}(p) = \delta_{ij}, \quad \frac{\partial g_{ij}}{\partial x^k}(p) = 0, \quad \Gamma^i_{jk}(p) = 0.$$

Therefore, the covariant derivative reduces to a partial derivative, and the geodesics through p are locally linear functions of t. This idea was implemented by Einstein in his General Relativity using his Equivalence Principle and understanding the _____ as an inertial frame.

a. Normal coordinates
b. Riemannian geometry
c. Cotton tensor
d. Riemannian circle

30   Chapter 2. Regular Surfaces

41. In mathematics, a _____ in a normed vector space is a vector (often a spatial vector) whose length is 1 (the unit length.) A _____ is often denoted by a lowercase letter with a superscribed caret or 'hat', like this: $\hat{\imath}$.

In Euclidean space, the dot product of two _____s is simply the cosine of the angle between them.

    a. Unit vector
    b. ADE classification
    c. Euclidean subspace
    d. AA postulate

42. A _____ to a flat surface is a vector which is perpendicular to that surface. A normal to a non-flat surface at a point P on the surface is a vector perpendicular to the tangent plane to that surface at P. The word 'normal' is also used as an adjective: a line normal to a plane, the normal component of a force, the normal vector, etc. The concept of normality generalizes to orthogonality.

    a. Developable surface
    b. Surface Normal
    c. Dupin cyclide
    d. Paraboloid

43. The _____, after the plane and the catenoid, is the third minimal surface to be known. It was first discovered by Jean Baptiste Meusnier in 1776. For every point on the _____ there is a helix contained in the _____ which passes through that point.

The _____ is shaped like Archimedes' screw, but extends infinitely in all directions. It can be described by the following parametric equations in Cartesian coordinates:

$$x = \rho \cos\theta$$
$$y = \rho \sin\theta$$
$$z = \alpha \theta$$

where ρ and θ range from negative infinity to positive infinity, while α is a constant. If α is positive then the _____ is right-handed; if negative then left-handed.

Chapter 2. Regular Surfaces

a. -module
b. Scherk surface
c. Weaire-Phelan structure
d. Helicoid

44. In mathematics, a _____ of a submanifold of a smooth manifold is an open set around it resembling the normal bundle.

The idea behind a _____ can be explained in a simple example. Consider a smooth curve in the plane without self-intersections.

a. 11-cell
b. 1-center problem
c. -module
d. Tubular neighborhood

45. In combinatorial mathematics, given a collection C of sets, a _____ is a set containing exactly one element from each member of the collection: it is a section of the quotient map induced by the collection. If the original sets are not disjoint, there are several different definitions. One variation is that there is a bijection f from the _____ to C such that x is an element of f(x) for each x in the _____.
a. Geometric combinatorics
b. No-three-in-line
c. Transversal
d. -module

46. In a totally ordered set all elements are mutually comparable, so such a set can have at most one minimal element and at most one maximal element. Then, due to mutual comparability, the minimal element will also be the least element and the maximal element will also be the greatest element. Thus in a totally ordered set we can simply use the terms minimum and _____.

a. -module
b. Maximum
c. Fresnel integrals
d. Hyperbolic angle

47. In calculus, the _____ is a formula for the derivative of the composite of two functions.

In intuitive terms, if a variable, y, depends on a second variable, u, which in turn depends on a third variable, x, then the rate of change of y with respect to x can be computed as the rate of change of y with respect to u multiplied by the rate of change of u with respect to x. Schematically,

a. -module
b. Chain rule
c. 11-cell
d. 1-center problem

48. In mathematics, _____ of order k of functions is an equivalence relation, corresponding to having the same value at a point P and also the same derivatives there, up to order k. The equivalence classes are generally called jets. The point of osculation is also called the double cusp.
  a. 1-center problem
  b. Contact
  c. 11-cell
  d. -module

49. A _____ is an instrument used in geometry, technical drawing and engineering/building to measure distances and/or to rule straight lines. Strictly speaking, the _____ is essentially a straightedge used to rule lines and the calibrated instrument used for determining measurement is called a 'measure'. However, common usage is that a _____ is a calibrated straightedge that can be used for making measurements.
  a. 1-center problem
  b. -module
  c. Ruler
  d. 11-cell

50. In differential geometry, the _____ is the inner product on the tangent space of a surface in three-dimensional Euclidean space which is induced canonically from the dot product of R^3. It permits the calculation of curvature and metric properties of a surface such as length and area in a manner consistent with the ambient space. The _____ is denoted by the Roman numeral I,

Let X(u, v) be a parametric surface.

Chapter 2. Regular Surfaces

a. Saddle point
b. Weingarten equations
c. Gauss map
d. First fundamental form

51. In mathematical analysis and related areas of mathematics, a set is called _____, if it is, in a certain sense, of finite size. Conversely a set which is not _____ is called unbounded.

A set S of real numbers is called _____ from above if there is a real number k such that k >≥ s for all s in S. The number k is called an upper bound of S. The terms _____ from below and lower bound are similarly defined.

a. -module
b. Bounded
c. 1-center problem
d. 11-cell

52. In the differential geometry of surfaces, an _____ is a curve always tangent to an asymptotic direction of the surface (where they exist.) It is sometimes called an asymptotic line, although it need not be a line.

An asymptotic direction is one in which the normal curvature is zero.

a. Asymptotic curve
b. Astroid
c. Isogonal trajectory
d. Ogive

53. In a group, the _____ by g of h is ghg^{-1}.

If h is a translation, then its _____ by an isometry can be described as applying the isometry to the translation:

- the _____ of a translation by a translation is the first translation
- the _____ of a translation by a rotation is a translation by a rotated translation vector
- the _____ of a translation by a reflection is a translation by a reflected translation vector

Thus the conjugacy class within the Euclidean group E(n) of a translation is the set of all translations by the same distance.

The smallest subgroup of the Euclidean group containing all translations by a given distance is the set of all translations. Thus this is the _____ closure of a singleton containing a translation.

   a. Conjugate
   b. -module
   c. 11-cell
   d. 1-center problem

54. In mathematics, a _____ is a collection of points which share a property. The term _____ is usually used of a condition which defines a continuous figure or figures, that is, a curve. For example, in two-dimensional space a line is the _____ of points equidistant from two fixed points or from two parallel lines.
   a. Locus
   b. 9-j symbols
   c. Barycentric coordinates
   d. Centered polygonal numbers

55. In geometry the _____ of a polyhedron is an arrangement of edge-joined polygons in the plane which can be folded (along edges) to become the faces of the polyhedron. Polyhedral _____s are a useful aid to the study of polyhedra and solid geometry in general, as they allow for models of polyhedra to be constructed from material such as thin cardboard.

It is a long-standing open question whether or not every convex polyhedron P (one without 'dents' - in other words, all dihedral angles between the edges are ≤ 180 degrees) has a _____: whether the surface P may be cut along edges and unfolded flat to a planar polygon (without overlap.)

   a. Five-pointed star
   b. Constructible polygon
   c. Hexagon
   d. Net

56. A _____ of a concept is an extension of the concept to less-specific criteria. It is a foundational element of logic and human reasoning. _____ posits the existence of a domain or set of elements, as well as one or more common characteristics shared by those elements.
   a. -module
   b. 11-cell
   c. Generalization
   d. 1-center problem

Chapter 2. Regular Surfaces

57. In mathematics, an _____ on a real vector space is a choice of which ordered bases are 'positively' oriented and which are 'negatively' oriented. In the three-dimensional Euclidean space, the two possible basis _____s are called right-handed and left-handed (or right-chiral and left-chiral), respectively. However, the choice of _____ is independent of the handedness or chirality of the bases (although right-handed bases are typically declared to be positively oriented, they may also be assigned a negative _____.)
   a. Adams-hemisphere-in-a-square
   b. Apex
   c. Apollonius' theorem
   d. Orientation

58. In mathematics, _____ is a property of surfaces in Euclidean space measuring whether or not it is possible to make a consistent choice of surface normal vector at every point. A choice of surface normal allows one to use the right-hand rule to define a 'clockwise' direction of loops in the surface, as needed by Stokes' theorem for instance. More generally, _____ of an abstract surface, or manifold, measures whether one can consistently choose a 'clockwise' orientation for all loops in the manifold.
   a. Exotic sphere
   b. Orbifold
   c. Orientability
   d. Unit tangent bundle

59. In mathematics, a topological space is called _____ if each of its open covers has a finite subcover. Otherwise it is called non-_____.

The Heine-Borel theorem shows that this definition is equivalent to 'closed and bounded' for subsets of Euclidean space. So a subset of Euclidean space R^n is called _____ if it is closed and bounded. For example, in R, the closed unit interval [0, 1] is _____, but the set of integers Z is not (it is not bounded) and neither is the half-open interval [0, 1) (it is not closed).

   a. 11-cell
   b. 1-center problem
   c. -module
   d. Compact

60. In formal mathematical logic, the concept of a _____ may be taken to mean a formula that can be derived according to the derivation rules of a fixed formal system. The statements of a theory as expressed in a formal language are called its elementary _____s and are said to be true.

The essential property of _____s is that they are derivable using a fixed set of inference rules and axioms without any additional assumptions.

Chapter 2. Regular Surfaces

a. Theorem
b. Rule of inference
c. Proof
d. Logical axioms

61. In mathematics, a _____ is the inside of a sphere; both concepts apply not only in the three-dimensional space but also for lower and higher dimensions, and for metric spaces in general.

Let (M,d) be a metric space, namely a set M with a metric (distance function) d. The open (metric) _____ of radius r > 0 centered at a point p in M, usually denoted by $B_r(p)$ or B(p;r), is defined by

The closed (metric) _____, which may be denoted by $B_r[p]$ or B[p;r], is defined by

Note in particular that a _____ always includes *p* itself, since the definition requires *r* > 0.

a. -module
b. Ball
c. 1-center problem
d. 11-cell

62. In mathematics, a continuous function is a function for which, intuitively, small changes in the input result in small changes in the output. Otherwise, a function is said to be _____. A continuous function with a continuous inverse function is called bicontinuous.
a. 1-center problem
b. 11-cell
c. Discontinuous
d. -module

63. In the mathematical field of topology, a _____ or topological isomorphism is a bicontinuous function between two topological spaces. _____s are the isomorphisms in the category of topological spaces -- that is, they are the mappings which preserve all the topological properties of a given space. Two spaces with a _____ between them are called homeomorphic, and from a topological viewpoint they are the same.

Chapter 2. Regular Surfaces

Roughly speaking, a topological space is a geometric object, and the _____ is a continuous stretching and bending of the object into a new shape. Thus, a square and a circle are homeomorphic to each other, but a sphere and a donut are not.

a. -module
b. 11-cell
c. 1-center problem
d. Homeomorphism

64. In mathematical analysis, the _____ states that for each value between the least upper bound and greatest lower bound of the image of a continuous function there is a corresponding value in its domain mapping to the original. _____

- Version I. The _____ states the following: If the function y = f(x) is continuous on the interval [a, b], and u is a number between f(a) and f(b), then there is a c >∈ [a, b] such that f(c) = u.

- Version II. Suppose that I is an interval [a, b] in the real numbers R and that f : I >→ R is a continuous function. Then the image set f(I) is also an interval, and either it contains [f(a), f(b)], or it contains [f(b), f(a)]; that is,

  >f(I) >⊇ [f(a), f(b)], or >f(I) >⊇ [f(b), f(a)].

It is frequently stated in the following equivalent form: Suppose that >f : [a, b] >→ R is continuous and that u is a real number satisfying >f(a) < u < f(b) or >f(a) > u > f(b.) Then for some c >∈ [a, b], f(c) = u.

a. Intermediate value theorem
b. ADHM construction
c. AA postulate
d. ADE classification

65. The _____, often simply called the Jacobian, is the determinant of the Jacobian matrix.

The _____ of a function describes the orientation of a tangent plane to the function at a given point. In this way, the _____ generalizes the gradient of a scalar valued function of multiple variables which itself generalizes the derivative of a scalar-valued function of a scalar.

a. 1-center problem
b. -module
c. 11-cell
d. Jacobian determinant

66. In vector calculus, the _____ is the matrix of all first-order partial derivatives of a vector-valued function. Suppose F : $R^n \rightarrow R^m$ is a function from Euclidean n-space to Euclidean m-space. Such a function is given by m real-valued component functions, $y_1(x_1,...,x_n)$, ..., $y_m(x_1,...,x_n)$.

a. Jacobian matrix
b. -module
c. 11-cell
d. 1-center problem

67. In mathematics, specifically differential calculus, the _____ gives sufficient conditions for a function to be invertible in a neighborhood of a point in its domain. The theorem also gives a formula for the derivative of the inverse function.

In multivariable calculus, this theorem can be generalized to any vector-valued function whose Jacobian determinant is nonzero at a point in its domain.

a. ADE classification
b. Inverse function theorem
c. AA postulate
d. Isoperimetric inequality

Chapter 3. The Geometry of the Gauss Map

1. In differential geometry, the _____ maps a surface in Euclidean space R^3 to the unit sphere S^2. Namely, given a surface X lying in R^3, the _____ is a continuous map N: X >→ S^2 such that N(p) is a unit vector orthogonal to X at p, namely the normal vector to X at p.

The _____ can be defined (globally) if and only if the surface is orientable, in which case its degree is half the Euler characteristic.

    a. Weingarten equations
    b. Gauss map
    c. Gauss-Codazzi equations
    d. Ridge

2. In mathematics, an _____ on a real vector space is a choice of which ordered bases are 'positively' oriented and which are 'negatively' oriented. In the three-dimensional Euclidean space, the two possible basis _____s are called right-handed and left-handed (or right-chiral and left-chiral), respectively. However, the choice of _____ is independent of the handedness or chirality of the bases (although right-handed bases are typically declared to be positively oriented, they may also be assigned a negative _____.)

    a. Apollonius' theorem
    b. Adams-hemisphere-in-a-square
    c. Orientation
    d. Apex

3. In mathematics, a _____ consists of the points through which a continuously moving point passes. This notion captures the intuitive idea of a geometrical one-dimensional object, which furthermore is connected in the sense of having no discontinuities or gaps. Simple examples include the sine wave as the basic _____ underlying simple harmonic motion, and the parabola.

    a. Dual curve
    b. Curve
    c. Sectrix of Maclaurin
    d. Singular point

4. A _____ is a visual representation of an area--a symbolic depiction highlighting relationships between elements of that space such as objects, regions, and themes.

Many _____s are static two-dimensional, geometrically accurate (or approximately accurate) representations of three-dimensional space, while others are dynamic or interactive, even three-dimensional. Although most commonly used to depict geography, _____s may represent any space, real or imagined, without regard to context or scale; e.g. Brain mapping, DNA mapping, and extraterrestrial mapping.

a. -module
b. 11-cell
c. Map
d. 1-center problem

5. In technical applications of 3D computer graphics (CAx) such as computer-aided design and computer-aided manufacturing, _____s are one way of representing objects. The other ways are wireframe (lines and curves) and solids. Point clouds are also sometimes used as temporary ways to represent an object, with the goal of using the points to create one or more of the three permanent representations.
   a. Space partitioning
   b. Geometric primitive
   c. Solid modeling
   d. Surface

6. In mathematics, _____ refers to any of a number of loosely related concepts in different areas of geometry. Intuitively, _____ is the amount by which a geometric object deviates from being flat, or straight in the case of a line, but this is defined in different ways depending on the context. There is a key distinction between extrinsic _____, which is defined for objects embedded in another space (usually a Euclidean space) in a way that relates to the radius of _____ of circles that touch the object, and intrinsic _____, which is defined at each point in a differential manifold.
   a. Stiefel manifold
   b. Second fundamental form
   c. Curvature
   d. Four-vertex theorem

7. In Riemannian geometry, the _____ at p consist of a chart such that locally the symmetric part of the Christoffel symbols vanish, i.e. $\Gamma^a_{(bc)} = 0$. Furthermore, at p, the following equations hold

$$g_{ij}(p) = \delta_{ij}, \quad \frac{\partial g_{ij}}{\partial x^k}(p) = 0, \quad \Gamma^i_{jk}(p) = 0.$$

Therefore, the covariant derivative reduces to a partial derivative, and the geodesics through p are locally linear functions of t. This idea was implemented by Einstein in his General Relativity using his Equivalence Principle and understanding the _____ as an inertial frame.

a. Riemannian circle
b. Riemannian geometry
c. Cotton tensor
d. Normal coordinates

8. In differential geometry, the _____ is a quadratic form on the tangent plane of a smooth surface in the three dimensional Euclidean space, usually denoted by II. Together with the first fundamental form, it serves to define extrinsic invariants of the surface, its principal curvatures. More generally, such a quadratic form is defined for a smooth hypersurface in a Riemannian manifold and a smooth choice of the unit normal vector at each point.

a. Second fundamental form
b. Lie derivative
c. G_2-structure
d. Pedal curve

9. A _____ is a number that determines the location of a point along some line or curve. A list of two, three, or more _____s can be used to determine the location of a point on a surface, volume, or higher-dimensional domain.

For example, the longitude is a _____ which determines the position of a point along the Earth's equator, and latitude is another _____ that defines a poisition along a meridian.

a. 11-cell
b. -module
c. 1-center problem
d. Coordinate

10. In the mathematical field of topology, a _____ of a fiber bundle, π: E → B, over a topological space, B, is a continuous map, s : B → E, such that π(s(x))=x for all x in B.

A _____ is a certain generalization of the notion of the graph of a function. The graph of a function g : X → Y can be identified with a function taking its values in the Cartesian product E = X×Y of X and Y:

$$s(x) = (x, g(x)) \in E, \quad s : X \to E.$$

A _____ is an abstract characterization of what it means to be a graph.

a. Pullback bundle
b. Circle bundle
c. Subbundle
d. Section

11. In formal mathematical logic, the concept of a _____ may be taken to mean a formula that can be derived according to the derivation rules of a fixed formal system. The statements of a theory as expressed in a formal language are called its elementary _____s and are said to be true.

The essential property of _____s is that they are derivable using a fixed set of inference rules and axioms without any additional assumptions.

a. Theorem
b. Logical axioms
c. Rule of inference
d. Proof

12. A _____ is one of the most curvilinear basic geometric shapes:It has two faces, zero vertices, and zero edges. The surface formed by the points at a fixed distance from a given straight line, the axis of the _____. The solid enclosed by this surface and by two planes perpendicular to the axis is also called a _____.

a. 1-center problem
b. Cylinder
c. Bounded
d. -module

13. In differential geometry, the two _____ at a given point of a surface measure how the surface bends by different amounts in different directions at that point.

At each point p of a differentiable surface in 3-dimensional Euclidean space one may choose a unit normal vector. A normal plane at p is one that contains the normal, and will therefore also contain a unique direction tangent to the surface and cut the surface in a plane curve.

a. Gaussian curvature
b. Principal curvatures
c. Geodesic curvature
d. Menger curvature

Chapter 3. The Geometry of the Gauss Map

14. In differential geometry, the _____ of a point on a surface is the product of the principal curvatures, κ_1 and κ_2, of the given point. It is an intrinsic measure of curvature, i.e., its value depends only on how distances are measured on the surface, not on the way it is embedded in space. This result is the content of Gauss's Theorema egregium.

Symbolically, the _____ K is defined as

$$K = \kappa_1 \kappa_2.$$

where κ_1 and κ_2 are the principal curvatures.

a. Principal curvatures
b. Gaussian curvature
c. Menger curvature
d. Geodesic curvature

15. In mathematics, the _____ H of a surface S is an extrinsic measure of curvature that comes from differential geometry and that locally describes the curvature of an embedded surface in some ambient space such as Euclidean space.

The concept was introduced by Sophie Germain in her work on elasticity theory.

Let p be a point on the surface S.

a. Hermitian symmetric space
b. Stiefel manifold
c. Covariant derivative
d. Mean curvature

16. In geometry, topology and related branches of mathematics a spatial _____ describes a specific object within a given space that consists of neither volume, area, length, nor any other higher dimensional analogue. Thus, a _____ is a 0-dimensional object. Because of their nature as one of the simplest geometric concepts, they are often used in one form or another as the fundamental constituents of geometry, physics, vector graphics, and many other fields.

a. 1-center problem
b. -module
c. Bounded
d. Point

Chapter 3. The Geometry of the Gauss Map

17. In mathematics, an _____ is the finite or bounded case of a conic section, the geometric shape that results from cutting a circular conical or cylindrical surface with an oblique plane. It is also the locus of all points of the plane whose distances to two fixed points add to the same constant.

_____s also arise as images of a circle or a sphere under parallel projection, and some cases of perspective projection.

   a. ADE classification
   b. AA postulate
   c. Ellipse
   d. ADHM construction

18. In differential geometry, an _____ on a regular surface in R^3 is a point p at which the Gaussian curvature $K(p) > 0$ or equivalently, the principal curvatures k_1 and k_2 have the same sign.
   a. Arc
   b. Exterior covariant derivative
   c. Omnitruncated 24-cell
   d. Elliptic Point

19. In the differential geometry of surfaces in three dimensions, umbilics or _____ are points which are locally spherical. At such points both principal curvatures are equal, and every tangent vector is a principal direction.

Umbilic points generally occur as isolated points in the elliptical region of the surface; that is, where the Gaussian curvature is positive.

   a. Absolutely convex sets
   b. Archimedes' circles
   c. Annulus
   d. Umbilical points

20. In the differential geometry of surfaces, an _____ is a curve always tangent to an asymptotic direction of the surface (where they exist.) It is sometimes called an asymptotic line, although it need not be a line.

An asymptotic direction is one in which the normal curvature is zero.

Chapter 3. The Geometry of the Gauss Map

a. Ogive
b. Isogonal trajectory
c. Astroid
d. Asymptotic curve

21. In the differential geometry of surfaces, an asymptotic curve is a curve always tangent to an _____ of the surface (where they exist.) It is sometimes called an asymptotic line, although it need not be a line.

An _____ is one in which the normal curvature is zero.

a. Epicycloid
b. Epitrochoid
c. Asymptotic direction
d. Epispiral

22. The _____ is a method for characterising the local shape of a surface. Draw a plane parallel to the tangent plane and a small distance away from it. Consider the intersection of the surface with this plane.
a. Dupin indicatrix
b. Dehn plane
c. Center of curvature
d. Bitruncated cubic honeycomb

23. In a group, the _____ by g of h is ghg^{-1}.

If h is a translation, then its _____ by an isometry can be described as applying the isometry to the translation:

- the _____ of a translation by a translation is the first translation
- the _____ of a translation by a rotation is a translation by a rotated translation vector
- the _____ of a translation by a reflection is a translation by a reflected translation vector

Thus the conjugacy class within the Euclidean group E(n) of a translation is the set of all translations by the same distance.

The smallest subgroup of the Euclidean group containing all translations by a given distance is the set of all translations. Thus this is the _____ closure of a singleton containing a translation.

46 Chapter 3. The Geometry of the Gauss Map

a. 11-cell
b. -module
c. 1-center problem
d. Conjugate

24. The _____ of a unit speed curve in differential geometry is given by taking a curve's tangent vectors as points, all of which must lie on the unit sphere. The movement of the _____ describes the changes in the original curves direction. If α is a unit speed curve, that is $\|\alpha'\| = 1$, and T is the unit tangent vector field along α, then the curve σ = T is the _____ of α.
   a. 1-center problem
   b. 11-cell
   c. -module
   d. Spherical image

25. In the elementary differential geometry of curves in three dimensions, the _____ of a curve measures how sharply it is twisting. Taken together, the curvature and the _____ of a space curve are analogous to the curvature of a plane curve. For example, they are coefficients in the system of differential equations for the Frenet frame given by the Frenet-Serret formulas.
   a. G-structure
   b. Symmetric space
   c. Darboux vector
   d. Torsion

26. In mathematics, a _____ is a generalization of the notion of a 'straight line' to 'curved spaces'. In the presence of a metric, _____s are defined to be (locally) the shortest path between points on the space. In the presence of an affine connection, _____s are defined to be curves whose tangent vectors remain parallel if they are transported along it.
   a. Gauge theory
   b. Volume
   c. Geodesic
   d. Minkowski space

27. In mathematics, two vectors are _____ if they are perpendicular, i.e., they form a right angle. The word comes from the Greek >á½€>ρ>θϊŒ>ς , meaning 'straight', and >>γ>ω>vī >α (gonia), meaning 'angle'. For example, a subway and the street above, although they do not physically intersect, are _____ if they cross at a right angle.

a. Interior algebra
b. Orthogonal
c. Algebraic K-theory
d. Embedding

28. In mathematics, the _____ is the surface defined by the equation

$$z = x^3 - 3xy^2.$$

It belongs to the class of saddle surfaces and its name derives from the observation that a saddle for a monkey requires three depressions: two for the legs, and one for the tail. The point (0,0,0) on the _____ corresponds to a degenerate critical point of the function z(x,y) at (0, 0.) The _____ has an isolated umbilic point with zero Gaussian curvature at the origin, while the curvature is strictly negative at all other points.

a. Critical point
b. Saddle surface
c. Hessian matrix
d. Monkey saddle

29. A _____ is a mathematical equation for an unknown function of one or several variables that relates the values of the function itself and its derivatives of various orders. _____s play a prominent role in engineering, physics, economics and other disciplines. Visualization of airflow into a duct modelled using the Navier-Stokes equations, a set of partial _____s.

_____s arise in many areas of science and technology; whenever a deterministic relationship involving some continuously changing quantities (modeled by functions) and their rates of change (expressed as derivatives) is known or postulated.

a. Differential equation
b. 11-cell
c. -module
d. 1-center problem

30. In mathematics, a _____ is an isomorphism of smooth manifolds. It is an invertible function that maps one differentiable manifold to another, such that both the function and its inverse are smooth. The image of a rectangular grid on a square under a _____ from the square onto itself.

Given two manifolds M and N, a bijective map f from M to N is called a _____ if both

$$f$$

and its inverse

$$f^{-1}$$

are differentiable (if these functions are r times continuously differentiable, f is called a C^r-_____.)

   a. Diffeomorphism
   b. 11-cell
   c. -module
   d. 1-center problem

31. A _____ is a three-dimensional shape made by rotating a catenary curve around the x axis. Not counting the plane, it is the first minimal surface to be discovered. It was found and proved to be minimal by Leonhard Euler in 1744.
   a. -module
   b. Catenoid
   c. Helicoid
   d. Weaire-Phelan structure

32. The _____, after the plane and the catenoid, is the third minimal surface to be known. It was first discovered by Jean Baptiste Meusnier in 1776. For every point on the _____ there is a helix contained in the _____ which passes through that point.

The _____ is shaped like Archimedes' screw, but extends infinitely in all directions. It can be described by the following parametric equations in Cartesian coordinates:

$$x$$

$$y$$

$$z$$

where ρ and θ range from negative infinity to positive infinity, while α is a constant. If α is positive then the _____ is right-handed; if negative then left-handed.

Chapter 3. The Geometry of the Gauss Map

a. Weaire-Phelan structure
b. -module
c. Scherk surface
d. Helicoid

33. The _____, are coordinate-space expressions for the Levi-Civita connection derived from the metric tensor. In broader sense, the connection coefficients of an arbitrary (not necessarily metric) affine connection in a coordinate basis are often called _____. The _____ may be used for performing practical calculations in differential geometry.

The _____ are defined by:

Definition

The _____ can be derived from the vanishing of the covariant derivative of the metric tensor:

As a shorthand notation, the nabla symbol and the partial derivative symbols are frequently dropped, and instead a semi-colon and a comma are used to set off the index that is being used for the derivative. Thus, the above is sometimes written as

a. Killing vector field
b. Cartan-Karlhede algorithm
c. Christoffel symbols
d. Hopf-Rinow theorem

34. In mathematics, _____ in differential geometry is a concept most commonly applied to surfaces. For those the scalar curvature is a single number determining the local geometry, and its constancy has the obvious meaning that it is the same at all points. The circle has _____, also, in a natural (but different) sense.

a. Klein geometry
b. Darboux frame
c. Constant curvature
d. Courant bracket

35. In mathematics, _____ of order k of functions is an equivalence relation, corresponding to having the same value at a point P and also the same derivatives there, up to order k. The equivalence classes are generally called jets. The point of osculation is also called the double cusp.

   a. 1-center problem
   b. 11-cell
   c. -module
   d. Contact

36. In differential geometry of curves, the _____ of a sufficiently smooth plane curve at a given point on the curve is the circle whose center lies on the inner normal line and whose curvature is the same as that of the given curve at that point. This circle, which is the one among all tangent circles at the given point that approaches the curve most tightly, was named circulum osculans by Leibniz.

The center and radius of the _____ at a given point are called center of curvature and radius of curvature of the curve at that point.

   a. AA postulate
   b. Osculating circle
   c. Incenter
   d. Incircle

37. A _____ is a simple shape of Euclidean geometry consisting of those points in a plane which are the same distance from a given point called the centre. The common distance of the points of a _____ from its center is called its radius.

_____s are simple closed curves which divide the plane into two regions, an interior and an exterior.

   a. Circle
   b. Gergonne point
   c. Circumcircle
   d. Circumscribed circle

Chapter 3. The Geometry of the Gauss Map 51

38. In mathematics, a _____ is a quadric surface of special kind. There are two kinds of _____s: elliptic and hyperbolic. The elliptic _____ is shaped like an oval cup and can have a maximum or minimum point.

   a. Steiner surfaces
   b. PDE surfaces
   c. Parametric surface
   d. Paraboloid

39. In every _____ there is a cuboid with all vertices tangent to the surface of said _____. It immediately becomes apparent that the cuboid inscribed in the _____ must be a cube with all vertices tangent to the surface of the _____.

Formula 1, shown below, finds the length of one side of the inscribed cube, and Formula 2 finds the volume of the inscribed cube.

   a. Cone
   b. Point group in two dimensions
   c. Circumference
   d. Sphere

40. In mathematics, a _____ is a point on the domain of a function where:

   - one dimension: the derivative (or slope of the line when visualized) is equal to zero or a point where the function ceases to be differentiable.
   - in general: there are two distinct concepts: either the derivative (Jacobian) vanishes, or it is not of full rank (or, in either case, the function is not differentiable); these agree in one dimension.

Note that in one dimension, a critical value or critical number x of function f is the domain element at which the derivative is zero or undefined, whereas the associated ordered pair (x, y) is the _____. In higher dimensions a critical value is in the range whereas a _____ is in the domain.

There are two situations in which a point becomes a _____ of a function of one variable. The first of which is that the value of the first derivative is equal to zero.

   a. Saddle surface
   b. Critical point
   c. Hessian matrix
   d. Monkey saddle

Chapter 3. The Geometry of the Gauss Map

41. In functional analysis and related areas of mathematics, _____ topological vector spaces or _____ spaces are examples of topological vector spaces (TVS) which generalize normed spaces. They can be defined as topological vector spaces whose topology is generated by translations of balanced, absorbent, convex sets. Alternatively they can be defined as a vector space with a family of seminorms, and a topology can be defined in terms of that family.
   a. -module
   b. 1-center problem
   c. 11-cell
   d. Locally convex

42. In geometry, a polygon can be either _____ or concave.

A _____ polygon is a simple polygon whose interior is a _____ set. The following properties of a simple polygon are all equivalent to convexity:

   - Every internal angle is less than 180 degrees.
   - Every line segment between two vertices remains inside or on the boundary of the polygon.

A simple polygon is strictly _____ if every internal angle is strictly less than 180 degrees. Equivalently, a polygon is strictly _____ if every line segment between two nonadjacent vertices of the polygon is strictly interior to the polygon except at its endpoints.

   a. Separating axis theorem
   b. Supporting hyperplane
   c. Convex
   d. Convex combination

43. In mathematical writing, the adjective _____ is used to modify technical terms which have multiple meanings. It indicates that the exclusive meaning of the term is to be understood. (More formally, one could say that this is the meaning which implies the other meanings.)
   a. 1-center problem
   b. -module
   c. 11-cell
   d. Strict

44. In mathematics a _____ is a construction in vector calculus which associates a vector to every point in a (locally) Euclidean space.

Chapter 3. The Geometry of the Gauss Map

_____s are often used in physics to model, for example, the speed and direction of a moving fluid throughout space, or the strength and direction of some force, such as the magnetic or gravitational force, as it changes from point to point.

In the rigorous mathematical treatment, (tangent) _____s are defined on manifolds as sections of a manifold's tangent bundle.

a. -module
b. 11-cell
c. Vector field
d. 1-center problem

45. In mathematics, a _____ is a flat surface. _____s can arise as subspaces of some higher dimensional space, as with the walls of a room, or they may enjoy an independent existence in their own right, as in the setting of Euclidean geometry
   a. Parallelogram law
   b. Pendent
   c. Simple polytope
   d. Plane

46. A _____ is the path a moving object follows through space. The object might be a projectile or a satellite, for example. It thus includes the meaning of orbit - the path of a planet, an asteroid or a comet as it travels around a central mass.
   a. 1-center problem
   b. -module
   c. 11-cell
   d. Trajectory

47. In mathematics, an _____ is a parametric curve that represents a specific solution to an ordinary differential equation or system of equations. If the differential equation is represented as a vector field or slope field, then the corresponding _____s are tangent to the field at each point.

_____s are known by various other names, depending on the nature and interpretation of the differential equation or vector field.

a. Information geometry
b. Isothermal coordinates
c. Affine curvature
d. Integral curve

48. The _____ is often met for the first time as an operation on a single real function of a single real variable. One of the simplest settings for generalizations is to vector valued functions of several variables (most often the domain forms a vector space as well.) This is the field of multivariable calculus.
   a. -module
   b. 11-cell
   c. Derivative
   d. 1-center problem

49. A _____ of a concept is an extension of the concept to less-specific criteria. It is a foundational element of logic and human reasoning. _____ posits the existence of a domain or set of elements, as well as one or more common characteristics shared by those elements.
   a. Generalization
   b. -module
   c. 11-cell
   d. 1-center problem

50. _____ is a concept used in the testing of engineering models. A model is said to have _____ with the real application if the two share geometric similarity, kinematic similarity and dynamic similarity. Similarity and _____ are interchangeable in this context.
   a. 1-center problem
   b. -module
   c. Bounded
   d. Similitude

51. The latus rectum (2l) is the chord parallel to the _____ and passing through the focus (or one of the two foci).

The semi-latus rectum (l) is half the latus rectum.

The focal parameter (p) is the distance from the focus (or one of the two foci) to the _____.

Chapter 3. The Geometry of the Gauss Map

a. -module
b. Directrix
c. Conic
d. 1-center problem

52. A surface is doubly ruled if through every one of its points there are two distinct lines that lie on the surface. The hyperbolic paraboloid and the hyperboloid of one sheet are doubly _____. The plane is the only surface which contains three distinct lines through each of its points.

a. Gaussian surface
b. Dupin cyclide
c. Spring
d. Ruled surfaces

53. In linear algebra, a (linear) _____ is a subset of a vector space that is closed under multiplication by positive scalars. In other words, a subset C of a real vector space V is a _____ if and only if >λx belongs to C for any x in C and any positive scalar >λ of V (or, more succintly, if and only if >λC = C for any positive scalar >λ.)

A _____ is said to be pointed if it includes the null vector (origin) 0; otherwise it is said to be blunt.

a. Prismatic surface
b. Cone
c. Centerpoint
d. Complex line

54. In differential geometry, a discipline within mathematics, a _____ is a subset of the tangent bundle of a manifold satisfying certain properties. _____s are used to build up notions of integrability, and specifically of a foliation of a manifold

a. Banach manifold
b. G_2-structure
c. Theorema Egregium
d. Distribution

55. In mathematics, a _____ is a surface with zero Gaussian curvature. That is, it is 'surface' that can be flattened onto a plane without distortion (i.e. 'stretching' or 'compressing'). Conversely, it is a surface which can be made by transforming a plane (i.e. 'folding', 'bending', 'rolling', 'cutting' and/or 'gluing').

56   Chapter 3. The Geometry of the Gauss Map

a. Parametric surface
b. Developable surface
c. Paraboloid
d. Ruled surfaces

56. In mathematics, an _____ of a family of manifolds (especially a family of curves) is a manifold that is tangent to each member of the family at some point.

The simplest formal expression for an _____ of curves in the (x,y)-plane is the pair of equations

$$\boxed{x}>$$

$$\boxed{x}>$$

where the family is implicitly defined by (1.) Obviously the family has to be 'nicely' -- differentiably -- indexed by t.

a. Invariant differential operator
b. Envelope
c. Affine differential geometry
d. Evolute

57. In geometry, the _____ line (or simply the _____) to a curve at a given point is the straight line that 'just touches' the curve at that point (in the sense explained more precisely below.) As it passes through the point of tangency, the _____ line is 'going in the same direction' as the curve, and in this sense it is the best straight-line approximation to the curve at that point. The same definition applies to space curves and curves in n-dimensional Euclidean space.

a. Cartan connection
b. Tangent
c. Metric signature
d. Measuring function

58. In mathematics, a _____ is a surface with a mean curvature of zero. These include, but are not limited to, surfaces of minimum area subject to various constraints.

Physical models of area-minimizing _____s can be made by dipping a wire frame into a soap solution, forming a soap film, which is a _____ whose boundary is the wire frame.

Chapter 3. The Geometry of the Gauss Map

a. Minimal surface
b. Ricci decomposition
c. Chern-Weil theory
d. Projective connection

59. In mathematics, specifically in differential geometry, _____ on a Riemannian manifold are local coordinates where the metric is conformal to the Euclidean metric. This means that in _____, the Riemannian metric locally has the form

$$[\text{image}]>$$

where $[\text{image}]>$ is a smooth function.

_____ on surfaces were first introduced by Gauss. Korn and Lichtenstein proved that _____ exist around any point on a two dimensional Riemannian manifold. On higher dimensional Riemannian manifolds a necessary and sufficient condition for their local existence is the vanishing of the Weyl tensor and the Cotton tensor.

a. Affine focal set
b. Isothermal coordinates
c. Envelope
d. Induced metric

60. For a surface in three dimension the _____, surface of centers or evolute is formed by taking the centers of the curvature spheres, which are the tangential spheres whose radii are the reciprocals of one of the principal curvatures at the point of tangency. Equivalently it is the surface formed by the centers of the circles which osculate the curvature lines.

As the principal curvatures are the eigenvalues of the second fundamental form, there are two at each point, and these give rise to two points of the _____ on each normal direction to the surface.

a. Focal surface
b. Cross-cap
c. Spring
d. Steiner surfaces

61. A _____ of a curve is the envelope of a family of congruent circles centered on the curve. It generalises the concept of _____ lines.

58   Chapter 3. The Geometry of the Gauss Map

It is sometimes called the offset curve but the term 'offset' often refers also to translation.

a. Trisectrix of Maclaurin
b. Cissoid
c. Cassini oval
d. Parallel

62. In mathematics, an _____, isometric isomorphism or congruence mapping is a distance-preserving isomorphism between metric spaces. Geometric figures which can be related by an _____ are called congruent.

They are often used in constructions where one space is embedded in another space. For instance, the completion of a metric space M involves an _____ from M into M', a quotient set of the space of Cauchy sequences on M. The original space M is thus isometrically isomorphic to a subspace of a complete metric space, and it is usually identified with this subspace.

a. Isometry
b. Identity function
c. One-to-one
d. AA postulate

63. In chemistry, the _____ molecular geometry describes the arrangement of three or more atoms placed at an expected bond angle of 180°. _____ organic molecules, e.g. acetylene, are often described by invoking sp orbital hybridization for the carbon centers. Many _____ molecules exist, prominent examples include CO_2, HCN, and xenon difluoride.
a. -module
b. 1-center problem
c. 11-cell
d. Linear

64. For each eigenvector of a linear transformation, there is a corresponding scalar value called an _____ for that vector, which determines the amount the eigenvector is scaled under the linear transformation. For example, an _____ of +2 means that the eigenvector is doubled in length and points in the same direction. An _____ of +1 means that the eigenvector is unchanged, while an _____ of >−1 means that the eigenvector is reversed in sense.
a. Angular momentum
b. AA postulate
c. Eigenvector
d. Eigenvalue

65. For each _____ of a linear transformation, there is a corresponding scalar value called an eigenvalue for that vector, which determines the amount the _____ is scaled under the linear transformation. For example, an eigenvalue of +2 means that the _____ is doubled in length and points in the same direction. An eigenvalue of +1 means that the _____ is unchanged, while an eigenvalue of >−1 means that the _____ is reversed in sense.
   a. Eigenvalue
   b. AA postulate
   c. Angular momentum
   d. Eigenvector

Chapter 4. The Intrinsic Geometry of Surfaces

1. In mathematics, an _____, isometric isomorphism or congruence mapping is a distance-preserving isomorphism between metric spaces. Geometric figures which can be related by an _____ are called congruent.

They are often used in constructions where one space is embedded in another space. For instance, the completion of a metric space M involves an _____ from M into M', a quotient set of the space of Cauchy sequences on M. The original space M is thus isometrically isomorphic to a subspace of a complete metric space, and it is usually identified with this subspace.

   a. One-to-one
   b. AA postulate
   c. Identity function
   d. Isometry

2. A _____ is one of the most curvilinear basic geometric shapes: It has two faces, zero vertices, and zero edges. The surface formed by the points at a fixed distance from a given straight line, the axis of the _____. The solid enclosed by this surface and by two planes perpendicular to the axis is also called a _____.

   a. -module
   b. Bounded
   c. 1-center problem
   d. Cylinder

3. In mathematics, a _____ is a flat surface. _____s can arise as subspaces of some higher dimensional space, as with the walls of a room, or they may enjoy an independent existence in their own right, as in the setting of Euclidean geometry

   a. Pendent
   b. Plane
   c. Parallelogram law
   d. Simple polytope

4. A _____ is a number that determines the location of a point along some line or curve. A list of two, three, or more _____s can be used to determine the location of a point on a surface, volume, or higher-dimensional domain.

For example, the longitude is a _____ which determines the position of a point along the Earth's equator, and latitude is another _____ that defines a poisition along a meridian.

   a. -module
   b. 11-cell
   c. Coordinate
   d. 1-center problem

Chapter 4. The Intrinsic Geometry of Surfaces

5. A _____ is a three-dimensional shape made by rotating a catenary curve around the x axis. Not counting the plane, it is the first minimal surface to be discovered. It was found and proved to be minimal by Leonhard Euler in 1744.

   a. -module
   b. Weaire-Phelan structure
   c. Helicoid
   d. Catenoid

6. In linear algebra, a (linear) _____ is a subset of a vector space that is closed under multiplication by positive scalars. In other words, a subset C of a real vector space V is a _____ if and only if λx belongs to C for any x in C and any positive scalar λ of V (or, more succinctly, if and only if $\lambda C = C$ for any positive scalar λ.)

   A _____ is said to be pointed if it includes the null vector (origin) 0; otherwise it is said to be blunt.

   a. Prismatic surface
   b. Cone
   c. Centerpoint
   d. Complex line

7. The _____, after the plane and the catenoid, is the third minimal surface to be known. It was first discovered by Jean Baptiste Meusnier in 1776. For every point on the _____ there is a helix contained in the _____ which passes through that point.

   The _____ is shaped like Archimedes' screw, but extends infinitely in all directions. It can be described by the following parametric equations in Cartesian coordinates:

   $$x >$$
   $$x >$$
   $$x >$$

   where ρ and θ range from negative infinity to positive infinity, while α is a constant. If α is positive then the _____ is right-handed; if negative then left-handed.

   a. -module
   b. Scherk surface
   c. Helicoid
   d. Weaire-Phelan structure

Chapter 4. The Intrinsic Geometry of Surfaces

8. In mathematics, a _____ is a function which preserves angles. In the most common case the function is between domains in the complex plane.

More formally, a map

is called conformal (or angle-preserving) at z_0 if it preserves oriented angles between curves through z_0, as well as their orientation, i.e. direction.

   a. Weyl tensor
   b. Riemannian geometry
   c. Vector flow
   d. Conformal map

9. A _____ is a visual representation of an area--a symbolic depiction highlighting relationships between elements of that space such as objects, regions, and themes.

Many _____s are static two-dimensional, geometrically accurate (or approximately accurate) representations of three-dimensional space, while others are dynamic or interactive, even three-dimensional. Although most commonly used to depict geography, _____s may represent any space, real or imagined, without regard to context or scale; e.g. Brain mapping, DNA mapping, and extraterrestrial mapping.

   a. 1-center problem
   b. -module
   c. 11-cell
   d. Map

10. In mathematics, specifically in differential geometry, _____ on a Riemannian manifold are local coordinates where the metric is conformal to the Euclidean metric. This means that in _____, the Riemannian metric locally has the form

where ☐ is a smooth function.

_____ on surfaces were first introduced by Gauss. Korn and Lichtenstein proved that _____ exist around any point on a two dimensional Riemannian manifold. On higher dimensional Riemannian manifolds a necessary and sufficient condition for their local existence is the vanishing of the Weyl tensor and the Cotton tensor.

   a. Induced metric
   b. Affine focal set
   c. Isothermal coordinates
   d. Envelope

11. In mathematics, a _____ consists of the points through which a continuously moving point passes. This notion captures the intuitive idea of a geometrical one-dimensional object, which furthermore is connected in the sense of having no discontinuities or gaps. Simple examples include the sine wave as the basic _____ underlying simple harmonic motion, and the parabola.
   a. Curve
   b. Sectrix of Maclaurin
   c. Singular point
   d. Dual curve

12. In differential geometry, the _____ maps a surface in Euclidean space R^3 to the unit sphere S^2. Namely, given a surface X lying in R^3, the _____ is a continuous map N: X >→ S^2 such that N(p) is a unit vector orthogonal to X at p, namely the normal vector to X at p.

The _____ can be defined (globally) if and only if the surface is orientable, in which case its degree is half the Euler characteristic.

   a. Gauss-Codazzi equations
   b. Gauss map
   c. Ridge
   d. Weingarten equations

13. In mathematics, two vectors are _____ if they are perpendicular, i.e., they form a right angle. The word comes from the Greek >á½€>ρ>θÏŒ>ς , meaning 'straight', and >>γ>ω>vῖ >α (gonia), meaning 'angle'. For example, a subway and the street above, although they do not physically intersect, are _____ if they cross at a right angle.

64   Chapter 4. The Intrinsic Geometry of Surfaces

   a. Interior algebra
   b. Algebraic K-theory
   c. Embedding
   d. Orthogonal

14. In geometry, the _____ is a particular mapping (function) that projects a sphere onto a plane. The projection is defined on the entire sphere, except at one point -- the projection point. Where it is defined, the mapping is smooth and bijective.
   a. -module
   b. Mercator projection
   c. 1-center problem
   d. Stereographic projection

15. In chemistry, the _____ molecular geometry describes the arrangement of three or more atoms placed at an expected bond angle of 180°. _____ organic molecules, e.g. acetylene, are often described by invoking sp orbital hybridization for the carbon centers. Many _____ molecules exist, prominent examples include CO_2, HCN, and xenon difluoride.
   a. 1-center problem
   b. 11-cell
   c. Linear
   d. -module

16. In technical applications of 3D computer graphics (CAx) such as computer-aided design and computer-aided manufacturing, _____s are one way of representing objects. The other ways are wireframe (lines and curves) and solids. Point clouds are also sometimes used as temporary ways to represent an object, with the goal of using the points to create one or more of the three permanent representations.
   a. Space partitioning
   b. Geometric primitive
   c. Solid modeling
   d. Surface

17. In geometry, the _____ line (or simply the _____) to a curve at a given point is the straight line that 'just touches' the curve at that point (in the sense explained more precisely below.) As it passes through the point of tangency, the _____ line is 'going in the same direction' as the curve, and in this sense it is the best straight-line approximation to the curve at that point. The same definition applies to space curves and curves in n-dimensional Euclidean space.

a. Cartan connection
b. Measuring function
c. Tangent
d. Metric signature

18. In mathematics, a _____ could be any function mapping a set X onto another set or onto itself. However, often the set X has some additional algebraic or geometric structure and the term '_____' refers to a function from X to itself which preserves this structure.

Examples include linear _____s and affine _____s such as rotations, reflections and translations.

a. 1-center problem
b. -module
c. Transformation
d. Codomain

19. In differential geometry, the _____ of a point on a surface is the product of the principal curvatures, >κ_1 and >κ_2, of the given point. It is an intrinsic measure of curvature, i.e., its value depends only on how distances are measured on the surface, not on the way it is embedded in space. This result is the content of Gauss's Theorema egregium.

Symbolically, the _____ >K is defined as

>.

where >κ_1 and >κ_2 are the principal curvatures.

a. Menger curvature
b. Geodesic curvature
c. Principal curvatures
d. Gaussian curvature

20. _____ is a concept used in the testing of engineering models. A model is said to have _____ with the real application if the two share geometric similarity, kinematic similarity and dynamic similarity. Similarity and _____ are interchangeable in this context.

66   Chapter 4. The Intrinsic Geometry of Surfaces

a. 1-center problem
b. -module
c. Bounded
d. Similitude

21. In mathematics, _____ refers to any of a number of loosely related concepts in different areas of geometry. Intuitively, _____ is the amount by which a geometric object deviates from being flat, or straight in the case of a line, but this is defined in different ways depending on the context. There is a key distinction between extrinsic _____, which is defined for objects embedded in another space (usually a Euclidean space) in a way that relates to the radius of _____ of circles that touch the object, and intrinsic _____, which is defined at each point in a differential manifold.

a. Four-vertex theorem
b. Stiefel manifold
c. Second fundamental form
d. Curvature

22. _____ exercise or '_____s' are a type of strength training in which the joint angle and muscle length do not change during contraction (compared to concentric or eccentric contractions, called dynamic/isotonic movements.) _____s are done in static positions, rather than being dynamic through a range of motion. The joint and muscle are either worked against an immovable force (overcoming _____) or are held in a static position while opposed by resistance (yielding _____.)

a. ADHM construction
b. AA postulate
c. ADE classification
d. Isometric

23. Two metric spaces X and Y are called isometric if there is an isometry from X to Y. The set of _____ from a metric space to itself forms a group with respect to function composition, called the isometry group.

- Any reflection, translation and rotation is a global isometry on Euclidean spaces.

- The map R ⎯→ R defined by ⎯→ is a path isometry but not a global isometry.

- The isometric linear maps from C^n to itself are the unitary matrices.

Chapter 4. The Intrinsic Geometry of Surfaces

Given two normed vector spaces V and W, a linear isometry is a linear map f : V >→ W that preserves the norms:

for all v in V. Linear _____ are distance-preserving maps in the above sense. They are global _____ if and only if they are surjective.

a. ADHM construction
b. AA postulate
c. ADE classification
d. Isometries

24. In mathematics, a _____ is a function between two vector spaces that preserves the operations of vector addition and scalar multiplication. The expression 'linear operator' is in especially common use, for _____s from a vector space to itself In advanced mathematics, the definition of linear function coincides with the definition of _____.
   a. 1-center problem
   b. -module
   c. 11-cell
   d. Linear Map

25. In mathematics, a _____ is an object of study in the abstract formulation of dynamical systems, and ergodic theory in particular.

A _____ is defined as a probability space and a measure-preserving transformation on it. In more detail, it is a system

Chapter 4. The Intrinsic Geometry of Surfaces

with the following structure:

- X is a set,
- ☐ is a σ-algebra over X,
- ☐ is a probability measure, so that $\mu(X) = 1$, and
- ☐ is a measurable transformation which preserves the measure μ, i. e. each ☐ satisfies

    ☐.

This definition can be generalized to the case in which T is not a single transformation that is iterated to give the dynamics of the system, but instead is a monoid (or even a group) of transformations ☐ parametrized by ☐ (or ☐, or ☐, or ☐), where each transformation T_s satisfies the same requirements as T above. In particular, the transformations obey the rules

- ☐, the identity function on X;
- ☐, whenever all the terms are well-defined;
- ☐, whenever all the terms are well-defined.

The earlier, simpler case fits into this framework by defining ☐ for ☐.

The existence of invariant measures for certain maps and Markov processes is established by the Krylov-Bogolyubov theorem.

a. Measure-preserving dynamical system
b. -module
c. 11-cell
d. 1-center problem

26. In mathematics, a _____ is an isomorphism of smooth manifolds. It is an invertible function that maps one differentiable manifold to another, such that both the function and its inverse are smooth. The image of a rectangular grid on a square under a _____ from the square onto itself.

Chapter 4. The Intrinsic Geometry of Surfaces

Given two manifolds M and N, a bijective map f from M to N is called a _____ if both

$f: M \to N$

and its inverse

$f^{-1}: N \to M$

are differentiable (if these functions are r times continuously differentiable, f is called a C^r-_____.)

a. 11-cell
b. 1-center problem
c. -module
d. Diffeomorphism

27. The _____ is a cylindrical map projection presented by the Flemish geographer and cartographer Gerardus Mercator, in 1569. It became the standard map projection for nautical purposes because of its ability to represent lines of constant course, known as rhumb lines or loxodromes, as straight segments. While the linear scale is constant in all directions around any point, thus preserving the angles and the shapes of small objects (which makes the projection conformal), the _____ distorts the size and shape of large objects, as the scale increases from the Equator to the poles, where it becomes infinite.

a. Stereographic projection
b. -module
c. 1-center problem
d. Mercator projection

28. In every _____ there is a cuboid with all vertices tangent to the surface of said _____. It immediately becomes apparent that the cuboid inscribed in the _____ must be a cube with all vertices tangent to the surface of the _____.

Formula 1, shown below, finds the length of one side of the inscribed cube, and Formula 2 finds the volume of the inscribed cube.

a. Cone
b. Circumference
c. Point group in two dimensions
d. Sphere

Chapter 4. The Intrinsic Geometry of Surfaces

29. The _____, are coordinate-space expressions for the Levi-Civita connection derived from the metric tensor. In broader sense, the connection coefficients of an arbitrary (not necessarily metric) affine connection in a coordinate basis are often called _____. The _____ may be used for performing practical calculations in differential geometry.

The _____ are defined by:

Definition

The _____ can be derived from the vanishing of the covariant derivative of the metric tensor:

As a shorthand notation, the nabla symbol and the partial derivative symbols are frequently dropped, and instead a semi-colon and a comma are used to set off the index that is being used for the derivative. Thus, the above is sometimes written as

a. Cartan-Karlhede algorithm
b. Hopf-Rinow theorem
c. Christoffel symbols
d. Killing vector field

30. A _____ is a surface created by rotating a curve lying on some plane (the generatrix) around a straight line (the axis of rotation) that lies on the same plane.

Examples of surfaces generated by a straight line are the cylindrical and conical surfaces. A circle that is rotated about a (coplanar) axis through the center generates a sphere.

a. -module
b. Definite integral
c. 1-center problem
d. Surface of revolution

Chapter 4. The Intrinsic Geometry of Surfaces

31. In formal mathematical logic, the concept of a _____ may be taken to mean a formula that can be derived according to the derivation rules of a fixed formal system. The statements of a theory as expressed in a formal language are called its elementary _____s and are said to be true.

The essential property of _____s is that they are derivable using a fixed set of inference rules and axioms without any additional assumptions.

  a. Proof
  b. Rule of inference
  c. Logical axioms
  d. Theorem

32. In geometry the _____ of a polyhedron is an arrangement of edge-joined polygons in the plane which can be folded (along edges) to become the faces of the polyhedron. Polyhedral _____s are a useful aid to the study of polyhedra and solid geometry in general, as they allow for models of polyhedra to be constructed from material such as thin cardboard.

It is a long-standing open question whether or not every convex polyhedron P (one without 'dents' - in other words, all dihedral angles between the edges are ≤ 180 degrees) has a _____: whether the surface P may be cut along edges and unfolded flat to a planar polygon (without overlap.)

  a. Five-pointed star
  b. Constructible polygon
  c. Hexagon
  d. Net

33. In mathematics, _____s are defined as a set of d coordinates $q = (q^1, q^2, ..., q^d)$ in which the coordinate surfaces all meet at right angles (note: superscripts are indices, not exponents.) A coordinate surface for a particular coordinate q^k is the curve, surface, or hypersurface on which q_k is a constant. For example, the three-dimensional Cartesian coordinates (x, y, z) is an _____ system, since its coordinate surfaces x=constant, y=constant, and z=constant are planes that meet at right angles to one another, i.e., are perpendicular.
  a. Elliptic cylindrical coordinates
  b. Oblate spheroidal coordinates
  c. Ellipsoidal coordinate
  d. Orthogonal coordinate

34. In mathematics, the _____ is a way of specifying a derivative along tangent vectors of a manifold. Alternatively, the _____ is a way of introducing and working with a connection on a manifold by means of a differential operator, to be contrasted with the approach given by a principal connection on the frame bundle -- see Affine connection

Chapter 4. The Intrinsic Geometry of Surfaces

a. Covariant derivative
b. Development
c. Connection form
d. Tortuosity

35. In mathematics a _____ is a construction in vector calculus which associates a vector to every point in a (locally) Euclidean space.

_____s are often used in physics to model, for example, the speed and direction of a moving fluid throughout space, or the strength and direction of some force, such as the magnetic or gravitational force, as it changes from point to point.

In the rigorous mathematical treatment, (tangent) _____s are defined on manifolds as sections of a manifold's tangent bundle.

a. 1-center problem
b. Vector field
c. 11-cell
d. -module

36. The _____ is often met for the first time as an operation on a single real function of a single real variable. One of the simplest settings for generalizations is to vector valued functions of several variables (most often the domain forms a vector space as well.) This is the field of multivariable calculus.

a. -module
b. 11-cell
c. 1-center problem
d. Derivative

37. A _____ of a curve is the envelope of a family of congruent circles centered on the curve. It generalises the concept of _____ lines.

It is sometimes called the offset curve but the term 'offset' often refers also to translation.

a. Trisectrix of Maclaurin
b. Cissoid
c. Parallel
d. Cassini oval

Chapter 4. The Intrinsic Geometry of Surfaces

38. In mathematics and logic, the phrase 'there is one and only one' is used to indicate that exactly one object with a certain property exists. In mathematical logic, this sort of quantification is known as _____ quantification or unique existential quantification.

_____ quantification is often denoted with the symbols '∃!' or '∃$_{=1}$'.

a. Uniqueness
b. ADE classification
c. ADHM construction
d. AA postulate

39. In mathematics, an _____ of a family of manifolds (especially a family of curves) is a manifold that is tangent to each member of the family at some point.

The simplest formal expression for an _____ of curves in the (x,y)-plane is the pair of equations

where the family is implicitly defined by (1.) Obviously the family has to be 'nicely' -- differentiably -- indexed by t.

a. Evolute
b. Affine differential geometry
c. Invariant differential operator
d. Envelope

40. A function or map from one topological space to another is called _____ if the inverse image of any open set is open. If the function maps the real numbers to the real numbers (both spaces with the Standard Topology), then this definition of _____ is equivalent to the definition of _____ in calculus. If a _____ function is one-to-one and onto and if the inverse of the function is also _____, then the function is called a homeomorphism and the domain of the function is said to be homeomorphic to the range.

a. Fresnel integrals
b. -module
c. Continuous
d. Metric space

74   Chapter 4. The Intrinsic Geometry of Surfaces

41. In mathematics, a _____ is a generalization of the notion of a 'straight line' to 'curved spaces'. In the presence of a metric, _____s are defined to be (locally) the shortest path between points on the space. In the presence of an affine connection, _____s are defined to be curves whose tangent vectors remain parallel if they are transported along it.

   a. Minkowski space
   b. Volume
   c. Gauge theory
   d. Geodesic

42. A _____ is a simple shape of Euclidean geometry consisting of those points in a plane which are the same distance from a given point called the centre. The common distance of the points of a _____ from its center is called its radius.

   _____s are simple closed curves which divide the plane into two regions, an interior and an exterior.

   a. Circumcircle
   b. Circumscribed circle
   c. Gergonne point
   d. Circle

43. In differential geometry, the _____ vector is a property of curves in a metric space which reflects the deviance of the curve from following the shortest arc length distance along each infinitesimal segment of its length.

   The vector is defined as follows: at a point P on a curve C, the _____ vector k_g is the curvature vector k of the projection of the curve C onto the tangent plane at P.

   The scalar magnitude of the _____ vector is simply called the _____ k_g.

   a. Gaussian curvature
   b. Geodesic Curvature
   c. Menger curvature
   d. Principal curvatures

44. A _____ is a mathematical equation for an unknown function of one or several variables that relates the values of the function itself and its derivatives of various orders. _____s play a prominent role in engineering, physics, economics and other disciplines. Visualization of airflow into a duct modelled using the Navier-Stokes equations, a set of partial _____s.

Chapter 4. The Intrinsic Geometry of Surfaces 75

_____s arise in many areas of science and technology; whenever a deterministic relationship involving some continuously changing quantities (modeled by functions) and their rates of change (expressed as derivatives) is known or postulated.

a. Differential equation
b. -module
c. 11-cell
d. 1-center problem

45. In mathematics, a _____ is a quadric surface of special kind. There are two kinds of _____s: elliptic and hyperbolic. The elliptic _____ is shaped like an oval cup and can have a maximum or minimum point.
a. Paraboloid
b. PDE surfaces
c. Parametric surface
d. Steiner surfaces

46. With a = b an elliptic paraboloid is a _____: a surface obtained by revolving a parabola around its axis. It is the shape of the parabolic reflectors used in mirrors, antenna dishes, and the like; and is also the shape of the surface of a rotating liquid, a principle used in liquid mirror telescopes. It is also called a circular paraboloid.
a. 11-cell
b. -module
c. 1-center problem
d. Paraboloid of revolution

47. In the elementary differential geometry of curves in three dimensions, the _____ of a curve measures how sharply it is twisting. Taken together, the curvature and the _____ of a space curve are analogous to the curvature of a plane curve. For example, they are coefficients in the system of differential equations for the Frenet frame given by the Frenet-Serret formulas.
a. G-structure
b. Torsion
c. Darboux vector
d. Symmetric space

48. An _____ is a type of quadric surface that is a higher dimensional analogue of an ellipse. The equation of a standard axis-aligned _____ body in an xyz-Cartesian coordinate system is

76 Chapter 4. The Intrinsic Geometry of Surfaces

$$\boxed{x}$$

where a and b are the equatorial radii (along the x and y axes) and c is the polar radius (along the z-axis), all of which are fixed positive real numbers determining the shape of the _____.

More generally, a not-necessarily-axis-aligned _____ is defined by the equation

$$\boxed{x}$$

where A is a symmetric positive definite matrix and x is a vector.

   a. ADE classification
   b. AA postulate
   c. ADHM construction
   d. Ellipsoid

49. In the mathematical field of differential geometry a _____ is a type of surface which in local coordinates may be written as a graph in R^3

   $z = f(x,y)$

such that the first fundamental form is of the form

$$\boxed{x}$$

Sometimes a metric of this form is called a Liouville metric. Every surface of revolution is a _____.

   a. Hexagonal prismatic honeycomb
   b. Positive current
   c. Cantitruncated 24-cell
   d. Liouville Surface

50. In a group, the _____ by g of h is ghg^{-1}.

If h is a translation, then its _____ by an isometry can be described as applying the isometry to the translation:

- the _____ of a translation by a translation is the first translation
- the _____ of a translation by a rotation is a translation by a rotated translation vector
- the _____ of a translation by a reflection is a translation by a reflected translation vector

Thus the conjugacy class within the Euclidean group E(n) of a translation is the set of all translations by the same distance.

The smallest subgroup of the Euclidean group containing all translations by a given distance is the set of all translations. Thus this is the _____ closure of a singleton containing a translation.

a. 11-cell
b. 1-center problem
c. -module
d. Conjugate

51. In mathematics, a _____ is a collection of points which share a property. The term _____ is usually used of a condition which defines a continuous figure or figures, that is, a curve. For example, in two-dimensional space a line is the _____ of points equidistant from two fixed points or from two parallel lines.

a. 9-j symbols
b. Centered polygonal numbers
c. Barycentric coordinates
d. Locus

52. A _____ is one of the basic shapes of geometry: a polygon with three corners or vertices and three sides or edges which are line segments. A _____ with vertices A, B, and C is denoted ABC.

In Euclidean geometry any three non-collinear points determine a unique _____ and a unique plane (i.e. a two-dimensional Euclidean space.)

a. -module
b. 1-center problem
c. Triangle
d. Brocard point

Chapter 4. The Intrinsic Geometry of Surfaces

53. In geometry and trigonometry, an _____ is the figure formed by two rays sharing a common endpoint, called the vertex of the _____ . The magnitude of the _____ is the 'amount of rotation' that separates the two rays, and can be measured by considering the length of circular arc swept out when one ray is rotated about the vertex to coincide with the other Where there is no possibility of confusion, the term '_____' is used interchangeably for both the geometric configuration itself and for its angular magnitude (which is simply a numerical quantity.)
   a. ADE classification
   b. ADHM construction
   c. AA postulate
   d. Angle

54. In geometry, an _____ is a closed segment of a differentiable curve in the two-dimensional plane; for example, a circular _____ is a segment of the circumference of a circle. If the _____ segment occupies a great circle (or great ellipse), it is considered a great-_____ segment.

   The length of an _____ of a circle with radius r and subtending an angle ⬚> (measured in radians) with the circle center -- i.e., the central angle -- equals ⬚>.

   a. Arc
   b. Equiangular polygon
   c. Almost symplectic manifold
   d. Order-4 dodecahedral honeycomb

55. In mathematics, an _____ on a real vector space is a choice of which ordered bases are 'positively' oriented and which are 'negatively' oriented. In the three-dimensional Euclidean space, the two possible basis _____s are called right-handed and left-handed (or right-chiral and left-chiral), respectively. However, the choice of _____ is independent of the handedness or chirality of the bases (although right-handed bases are typically declared to be positively oriented, they may also be assigned a negative _____.)
   a. Apollonius' theorem
   b. Adams-hemisphere-in-a-square
   c. Apex
   d. Orientation

56. In geometry, _____ is a way of transporting geometrical data along smooth curves in a manifold. If the manifold is equipped with an affine connection (a covariant derivative or connection on the tangent bundle), then this connection allows one to transport vectors of the manifold along curves so that they stay parallel with respect to the connection. Other notions of connection come equipped with their own parallel transportation systems as well.

Chapter 4. The Intrinsic Geometry of Surfaces

a. Parallel transport
b. Minimal volume
c. Riemannian circle
d. Riemannian geometry

57. Topology includes many subfields. The most basic and traditional division within topology is point-set topology, which establishes the foundational aspects of topology and investigates concepts inherent to _____ spaces - basic examples being compactness and connectedness; algebraic topology, which generally tries to measure degrees of connectivity using algebraic constructs such as homotopy groups and homology; and geometric topology, which primarily studies manifolds and their embeddings (placements) in other manifolds. Some of the most active areas, such as low dimensional topology and graph theory, do not fit neatly in this division.

a. 11-cell
b. -module
c. 1-center problem
d. Topological

58. In mathematics, and more specifically in algebraic topology and polyhedral combinatorics, the _____ is a topological invariant, a number that describes a topological space's shape or structure regardless of the way it is bent. It is commonly denoted by >χ '>chi).

The _____ was originally defined for polyhedra and used to prove various theorems about them, including the classification of the Platonic solids.

a. Abstract polytope
b. Alexander duality
c. Euler characteristic
d. Essential manifold

59. In mathematics, _____ has a few different, but closely related, meanings:

The _____ of a connected, orientable surface is an integer representing the maximum number of cuttings along closed simple curves without rendering the resultant manifold disconnected. It is equal to the number of handles on it. Alternatively, it can be defined in terms of the Euler characteristic >χ, via the relationship >χ = 2 >− 2g for closed surfaces, where g is the _____.

Chapter 4. The Intrinsic Geometry of Surfaces

a. Verdier duality
b. Clutching construction
c. Genus
d. Geometry and topology

60. In mathematics, the _____ of a set S consists of all points of S that are intuitively 'not on the edge of S'. A point that is in the _____ of S is an _____ point of S.

The exterior of a set is the _____ of its complement; it consists of the points that are not in the set or its boundary.

The notion of the _____ of a set is a topological concept; it is not defined for all sets, but it is defined for sets that are a subset of a topological space.

a. AA postulate
b. ADE classification
c. ADHM construction
d. Interior

61. In geometry, an _____ is an angle formed by two sides of a simple polygon that share an endpoint, namely, the angle on the inner side of the polygon. A simple polygon has exactly one internal angle per vertex.

If every _____ of a polygon is less than 180>°, the polygon is called convex.

a. Apollonius' theorem
b. Angle bisectors
c. Annulus
d. Interior Angle

62. In Riemannian geometry, the _____ at p consist of a chart such that locally the symmetric part of the Christoffel symbols vanish, i.e. $\Gamma^a_{(bc)} = 0$. Furthermore, at p, the following equations hold

$$g_{ij}(p) = \delta_{ij}, \quad \frac{\partial g_{ij}}{\partial x^k}(p) = 0, \quad \Gamma^i_{jk}(p) = 0.$$

Therefore, the covariant derivative reduces to a partial derivative, and the geodesics through p are locally linear functions of t. This idea was implemented by Einstein in his General Relativity using his Equivalence Principle and understanding the _____ as an inertial frame.

Chapter 4. The Intrinsic Geometry of Surfaces

a. Cotton tensor
b. Riemannian circle
c. Riemannian geometry
d. Normal coordinates

63. A _____ on a curve is one where it is not smooth, for example, at a cusp.

The precise definition of a _____ depends on the type of curve being studied.

Algebraic curves in R^2 are defined as the zero set $f^{-1}(0)$ for a polynomial function $f:R^2 \to R$.

a. Secant line
b. Sextic plane curve
c. Bicorn
d. Singular point

64. The _____ of a unit speed curve in differential geometry is given by taking a curve's tangent vectors as points, all of which must lie on the unit sphere. The movement of the _____ describes the changes in the original curves direction. If α is a unit speed curve, that is $\|\alpha'\| = 1$, and T is the unit tangent vector field along α, then the curve σ = T is the _____ of α.

a. 1-center problem
b. -module
c. 11-cell
d. Spherical image

65. In the field of mathematical logic, a clear distinction is made between two notions of _____s: logical _____s and non-logical _____s (somewhat similar to the ancient distinction between '_____s' and 'postulates' respectively)

These are certain formulas in a formal language that are universally valid, that is, formulas that are satisfied by every assignment of values. Usually one takes as logical _____s at least some minimal set of tautologies that is sufficient for proving all tautologies in the language; in the case of predicate logic more logical _____s than that are required, in order to prove logical truths that are not tautologies in the strict sense.

Chapter 4. The Intrinsic Geometry of Surfaces

In propositional logic it is common to take as logical _____s all formulae of the following forms, where φ, χ, and ψ can be any formulae of the language and where the included primitive connectives are only '¬' for negation of the immediately following proposition and '→' for implication from antecedent to consequent propositions:

1. $\phi \to (\psi \to \phi)$
2. $(\phi \to (\psi \to \chi)) \to ((\phi \to \psi) \to (\phi \to \chi))$
3. $(\neg\phi \to \neg\psi) \to (\psi \to \phi).$

Each of these patterns is an _____ schema, a rule for generating an infinite number of _____s. For example, if A, B, and C are propositional variables, then $A \to (B \to A)$ and $(A \to \neg B) \to (C \to (A \to \neg B))$ are both instances of _____ schema 1, and hence are _____s.

a. Axiom
b. ADE classification
c. Inductive reasoning
d. AA postulate

66. In geometry, topology and related branches of mathematics a spatial _____ describes a specific object within a given space that consists of neither volume, area, length, nor any other higher dimensional analogue. Thus, a _____ is a 0-dimensional object. Because of their nature as one of the simplest geometric concepts, they are often used in one form or another as the fundamental constituents of geometry, physics, vector graphics, and many other fields.

a. 1-center problem
b. Point
c. -module
d. Bounded

67. In differential geometry, the _____ is a generalization of the ordinary exponential function of mathematical analysis to all differentiable manifolds with an affine connection. Two important special cases of this are the _____ for a manifold with a Riemannian metric, and the _____ from a Lie algebra to a Lie group.

a. Orthogonal group
b. One-parameter group
c. Indefinite orthogonal group
d. Exponential map

Chapter 4. The Intrinsic Geometry of Surfaces

68. f>'(x) is twice the absolute value function, and it does not have a derivative at zero. Similar examples show that a function can have k derivatives for any non-negative integer k but no (k + 1)-order derivative. A function that has k successive derivatives is called _____.

a. 11-cell
b. 1-center problem
c. -module
d. K times differentiable

69. In mathematics, the _____ system is a two-dimensional coordinate system in which each point on a plane is determined by a distance from a fixed point and an angle from a fixed direction.

The fixed point (analogous to the origin of a Cartesian system) is called the pole, and the ray from the pole with the fixed direction is the polar axis. The distance from the pole is called the radial coordinate or radius, and the angle is the angular coordinate, polar angle, or azimuth.

a. 11-cell
b. 1-center problem
c. -module
d. Polar coordinate

70. In differential geometry, the _____ is the inner product on the tangent space of a surface in three-dimensional Euclidean space which is induced canonically from the dot product of R^3. It permits the calculation of curvature and metric properties of a surface such as length and area in a manner consistent with the ambient space. The _____ is denoted by the Roman numeral I,

Let X(u, v) be a parametric surface.

a. Gauss map
b. Weingarten equations
c. Saddle point
d. First fundamental form

71. The _____ is a geometric inequality involving the square of the circumference of a closed curve in the plane and the area of a plane region it encloses, as well as its various generalizations. Isoperimetric literally means 'having the same perimeter'. The isoperimetric problem is to determine a plane figure of the largest possible area whose boundary has a specified length.

Chapter 4. The Intrinsic Geometry of Surfaces

a. Inverse function theorem
b. Isoperimetric inequality
c. ADE classification
d. AA postulate

72. In mathematics, an _____ is a statement about the relative size or order of two objects, or about whether they are the same or not

- The notation a < b means that a is less than b.
- The notation a > b means that a is greater than b.
- The notation a ≠ b means that a is not equal to b, but does not say that one is bigger than the other or even that they can be compared in size.

In all these cases, a is not equal to b, hence, '_____'.

These relations are known as strict _____

- The notation a ≤ b means that a is less than or equal to b (or, equivalently, not greater than b);
- The notation a ≥ b means that a is greater than or equal to b (or, equivalently, not smaller than b);

An additional use of the notation is to show that one quantity is much greater than another, normally by several orders of magnitude.

- The notation a .

a. AA postulate
b. ADHM construction
c. Inequality
d. ADE classification

73. One of the meanings of the terms _____ and _____ transformation (also called dilation) of a Euclidean space is a function f from the space into itself that multiplies all distances by the same positive scalar r, so that for any two points x and y we have

$$d(f(x), f(y)) = rd(x, y),$$

where 'd(x,y)' is the Euclidean distance from x to y. Two sets are called similar if one is the image of the other under such a _____.

A special case is a homothetic transformation or central _____: it neither involves rotation nor taking the mirror image.

Chapter 4. The Intrinsic Geometry of Surfaces

a. Similarity
b. Flat
c. Similar
d. Square lattice

74. In differential geometry, the _____ of a connection on a smooth manifold is a general geometrical consequence of the curvature of the connection measuring the extent to which parallel transport around closed loops fails to preserve the geometrical data being transported. For flat connections, the associated _____ is a type of monodromy, and is an inherently global notion. For curved connections, _____ has nontrivial local and global features.

a. Holonomy
b. Differential geometry of curves
c. Connection form
d. G_2-structure

75. In geometry, a polygon can be either _____ or concave.

A _____ polygon is a simple polygon whose interior is a _____ set. The following properties of a simple polygon are all equivalent to convexity:

- Every internal angle is less than 180 degrees.
- Every line segment between two vertices remains inside or on the boundary of the polygon.

A simple polygon is strictly _____ if every internal angle is strictly less than 180 degrees. Equivalently, a polygon is strictly _____ if every line segment between two nonadjacent vertices of the polygon is strictly interior to the polygon except at its endpoints.

a. Convex combination
b. Separating axis theorem
c. Supporting hyperplane
d. Convex

76. In geometry, the notion of a _____ makes precise the idea of transporting data along a curve or family of curves in a parallel and consistent manner. There are a variety of kinds of _____s in modern geometry, depending on what sort of data one wants to transport. For instance, an affine _____, the most elementary type of _____, gives a means for transporting tangent vectors to a manifold from one point to another along a curve.

Chapter 4. The Intrinsic Geometry of Surfaces

a. Connection
b. Covariant derivative
c. Caustic
d. Finsler manifold

77. In the mathematical theory of Riemannian geometry, _____ are local coordinates that are adapted to a geodesic.

More formally, suppose M is an n-dimensional Riemannian manifold, >γ is a geodesic on M, and p is a point on >γ. Then there exists local coordinates [x] > around p such that:

- For small t, [x] > represents the geodesic near p,
- On >γ, the metric tensor is the Euclidean metric,
- On >γ, all Christoffel symbols vanish.

a. Nash embedding theorem
b. Seifert-Weber space
c. Fermi coordinates
d. Normal coordinates

78. For some curves there is a smallest number L that is an upper bound on the length of any polygonal approximation. If such a number exists, then the curve is said to be rectifiable and the curve is defined to have _____ L.

Let C be a curve in Euclidean (or, more generally, a metric) space X = R^n, so C is the image of a continuous function f : [a, b] >→ X of the interval [a, b] into X.

a. Arc length
b. ADE classification
c. ADHM construction
d. AA postulate

Chapter 5. Global Differential Geometry 87

1. In Riemannian geometry, a _____ is a vector field along a geodesic >γ in a Riemannian manifold describing the difference between the geodesic and an 'infinitesimally close' geodesic. In other words, the _____s along a geodesic form the tangent space to the geodesic in the space of all geodesics. They are named after Carl Jacobi.
    a. Weyl tensor
    b. Spin structure
    c. Harmonic map
    d. Jacobi field

2. In technical applications of 3D computer graphics (CAx) such as computer-aided design and computer-aided manufacturing, _____s are one way of representing objects. The other ways are wireframe (lines and curves) and solids. Point clouds are also sometimes used as temporary ways to represent an object, with the goal of using the points to create one or more of the three permanent representations.
    a. Surface
    b. Solid modeling
    c. Space partitioning
    d. Geometric primitive

3. In every _____ there is a cuboid with all vertices tangent to the surface of said _____. It immediately becomes apparent that the cuboid inscribed in the _____ must be a cube with all vertices tangent to the surface of the _____.

    Formula 1, shown below, finds the length of one side of the inscribed cube, and Formula 2 finds the volume of the inscribed cube.

    a. Cone
    b. Point group in two dimensions
    c. Circumference
    d. Sphere

4. The _____, are coordinate-space expressions for the Levi-Civita connection derived from the metric tensor. In broader sense, the connection coefficients of an arbitrary (not necessarily metric) affine connection in a coordinate basis are often called _____. The _____ may be used for performing practical calculations in differential geometry.

    The _____ are defined by:

    $\boxed{x}$>

    Definition

The _____ can be derived from the vanishing of the covariant derivative of the metric tensor g:

As a shorthand notation, the nabla symbol and the partial derivative symbols are frequently dropped, and instead a semi-colon and a comma are used to set off the index that is being used for the derivative. Thus, the above is sometimes written as

a. Cartan-Karlhede algorithm
b. Hopf-Rinow theorem
c. Killing vector field
d. Christoffel symbols

5. In mathematics, _____ in differential geometry is a concept most commonly applied to surfaces. For those the scalar curvature is a single number determining the local geometry, and its constancy has the obvious meaning that it is the same at all points. The circle has _____, also, in a natural (but different) sense.
   a. Courant bracket
   b. Klein geometry
   c. Darboux frame
   d. Constant curvature

6. In mathematics, _____ refers to any of a number of loosely related concepts in different areas of geometry. Intuitively, _____ is the amount by which a geometric object deviates from being flat, or straight in the case of a line, but this is defined in different ways depending on the context. There is a key distinction between extrinsic _____, which is defined for objects embedded in another space (usually a Euclidean space) in a way that relates to the radius of _____ of circles that touch the object, and intrinsic _____, which is defined at each point in a differential manifold.
   a. Second fundamental form
   b. Curvature
   c. Four-vertex theorem
   d. Stiefel manifold

7. In linear algebra, a (linear) _____ is a subset of a vector space that is closed under multiplication by positive scalars. In other words, a subset C of a real vector space V is a _____ if and only if >λx belongs to C for any x in C and any positive scalar >λ of V (or, more succinctly, if and only if >λC = C for any positive scalar >λ.)

A _____ is said to be pointed if it includes the null vector (origin) 0; otherwise it is said to be blunt.

a. Complex line
b. Centerpoint
c. Prismatic surface
d. Cone

8. In mathematics, a _____ consists of the points through which a continuously moving point passes. This notion captures the intuitive idea of a geometrical one-dimensional object, which furthermore is connected in the sense of having no discontinuities or gaps. Simple examples include the sine wave as the basic _____ underlying simple harmonic motion, and the parabola.

a. Dual curve
b. Singular point
c. Curve
d. Sectrix of Maclaurin

9. A function or map from one topological space to another is called _____ if the inverse image of any open set is open. If the function maps the real numbers to the real numbers (both spaces with the Standard Topology), then this definition of _____ is equivalent to the definition of _____ in calculus. If a _____ function is one-to-one and onto and if the inverse of the function is also _____, then the function is called a homeomorphism and the domain of the function is said to be homeomorphic to the range.

a. -module
b. Metric space
c. Fresnel integrals
d. Continuous

10. In mathematics, a _____ is a generalization of the notion of a 'straight line' to 'curved spaces'. In the presence of a metric, _____s are defined to be (locally) the shortest path between points on the space. In the presence of an affine connection, _____s are defined to be curves whose tangent vectors remain parallel if they are transported along it.

a. Geodesic
b. Volume
c. Gauge theory
d. Minkowski space

11. In formal mathematical logic, the concept of a _____ may be taken to mean a formula that can be derived according to the derivation rules of a fixed formal system. The statements of a theory as expressed in a formal language are called its elementary _____s and are said to be true.

Chapter 5. Global Differential Geometry

The essential property of _____s is that they are derivable using a fixed set of inference rules and axioms without any additional assumptions.

a. Rule of inference
b. Proof
c. Logical axioms
d. Theorem

12. In mathematics, a _____, named after Augustin Cauchy, is a sequence whose elements become arbitrarily close to each other as the sequence progresses. To be more precise, by dropping enough (but still only a finite number of) terms from the start of the sequence, it is possible to make the maximum of the distances from any of the remaining elements to any other such element smaller than any preassigned, necessarily positive, value.

In other words, suppose a pre-assigned positive real value ⬚> is chosen.

a. Hutchinson metric
b. Wijsman convergence
c. Gromov product
d. Cauchy sequence

13. In mathematics, a _____ is an ordered list of objects Like a set, it contains members, and the number of terms is called the length of the _____. Unlike a set, order matters, and the exact same elements can appear multiple times at different positions in the _____.
a. Slope
b. Slope of a line
c. Sequence
d. -module

14. In mathematics a _____ is a construction in vector calculus which associates a vector to every point in a (locally) Euclidean space.

_____s are often used in physics to model, for example, the speed and direction of a moving fluid throughout space, or the strength and direction of some force, such as the magnetic or gravitational force, as it changes from point to point.

In the rigorous mathematical treatment, (tangent) _____s are defined on manifolds as sections of a manifold's tangent bundle.

Chapter 5. Global Differential Geometry 91

   a. 1-center problem
   b. 11-cell
   c. -module
   d. Vector field

15. A _____ is a visual representation of an area--a symbolic depiction highlighting relationships between elements of that space such as objects, regions, and themes.

Many _____s are static two-dimensional, geometrically accurate (or approximately accurate) representations of three-dimensional space, while others are dynamic or interactive, even three-dimensional. Although most commonly used to depict geography, _____s may represent any space, real or imagined, without regard to context or scale; e.g. Brain mapping, DNA mapping, and extraterrestrial mapping.

   a. -module
   b. 1-center problem
   c. 11-cell
   d. Map

16. In geometry, an _____ is a closed segment of a differentiable curve in the two-dimensional plane; for example, a circular _____ is a segment of the circumference of a circle. If the _____ segment occupies a great circle (or great ellipse), it is considered a great-_____ segment.

The length of an _____ of a circle with radius r and subtending an angle θ (measured in radians) with the circle center -- i.e., the central angle -- equals θ.

   a. Arc
   b. Almost symplectic manifold
   c. Order-4 dodecahedral honeycomb
   d. Equiangular polygon

17. For some curves there is a smallest number L that is an upper bound on the length of any polygonal approximation. If such a number exists, then the curve is said to be rectifiable and the curve is defined to have _____ L.

Let C be a curve in Euclidean (or, more generally, a metric) space X = R^n, so C is the image of a continuous function f : [a, b] >→ X of the interval [a, b] into X.

Chapter 5. Global Differential Geometry

a. ADHM construction
b. ADE classification
c. AA postulate
d. Arc length

18. In mathematics, two vectors are _____ if they are perpendicular, i.e., they form a right angle. The word comes from the Greek >á½€>p>θïŒ>ς , meaning 'straight', and >>γ>ω>vī >α (gonia), meaning 'angle'. For example, a subway and the street above, although they do not physically intersect, are _____ if they cross at a right angle.
a. Embedding
b. Orthogonal
c. Interior algebra
d. Algebraic K-theory

19. A vector field J along a geodesic γ is said to be a Jacobi field if it satisfies the _____:

$$\frac{D^2}{dt^2}J(t) + R(J(t), \dot{\gamma}(t))\dot{\gamma}(t) = 0,$$

where D denotes the covariant derivative with respect to the Levi-Civita connection, R the Riemann curvature tensor, and $\dot{\gamma}(t) = d\gamma(t)/dt$ and t is the parameter of the geodesic. On a complete Riemannian manifold, for any Jacobi field there is a family of geodesics γ_τ describing the field (as in the preceding paragraph.)

The _____ is a linear, second order ordinary differential equation; in particular, values of J and $\frac{D}{dt}J$ at one point of γ uniquely determine the Jacobi field.

a. -module
b. 1-center problem
c. Jacobi equation
d. 11-cell

20. In a group, the _____ by g of h is ghg^{-1}.

Chapter 5. Global Differential Geometry

If h is a translation, then its _____ by an isometry can be described as applying the isometry to the translation:

- the _____ of a translation by a translation is the first translation
- the _____ of a translation by a rotation is a translation by a rotated translation vector
- the _____ of a translation by a reflection is a translation by a reflected translation vector

Thus the conjugacy class within the Euclidean group E(n) of a translation is the set of all translations by the same distance.

The smallest subgroup of the Euclidean group containing all translations by a given distance is the set of all translations. Thus this is the _____ closure of a singleton containing a translation.

a. -module
b. Conjugate
c. 11-cell
d. 1-center problem

21. In differential geometry, _____ are, roughly, points that can almost be joined by a 1-parameter family of geodesics. For example, on a sphere, the north-pole and south-pole are connected by any meridian.

Suppose p and q are points on a Riemannian manifold, and >γ is a geodesic that connects p and q.

a. Conjugate points
b. Vector flow
c. Filling radius
d. Space form

22. In geometry, topology and related branches of mathematics a spatial _____ describes a specific object within a given space that consists of neither volume, area, length, nor any other higher dimensional analogue. Thus, a _____ is a 0-dimensional object. Because of their nature as one of the simplest geometric concepts, they are often used in one form or another as the fundamental constituents of geometry, physics, vector graphics, and many other fields.

a. Bounded
b. 1-center problem
c. -module
d. Point

Chapter 5. Global Differential Geometry

23. In mathematics, a _____ is a collection of points which share a property. The term _____ is usually used of a condition which defines a continuous figure or figures, that is, a curve. For example, in two-dimensional space a line is the _____ of points equidistant from two fixed points or from two parallel lines.
    a. Barycentric coordinates
    b. 9-j symbols
    c. Centered polygonal numbers
    d. Locus

24. In mathematics, a _____ is a point on the domain of a function where:

    - one dimension: the derivative (or slope of the line when visualized) is equal to zero or a point where the function ceases to be differentiable.
    - in general: there are two distinct concepts: either the derivative (Jacobian) vanishes, or it is not of full rank (or, in either case, the function is not differentiable); these agree in one dimension.

    Note that in one dimension, a critical value or critical number x of function f is the domain element at which the derivative is zero or undefined, whereas the associated ordered pair (x, y) is the _____. In higher dimensions a critical value is in the range whereas a _____ is in the domain.

    There are two situations in which a point becomes a _____ of a function of one variable. The first of which is that the value of the first derivative is equal to zero.

    a. Saddle surface
    b. Monkey saddle
    c. Hessian matrix
    d. Critical Point

25. In mathematics, a _____ is a quadric surface of special kind. There are two kinds of _____s: elliptic and hyperbolic. The elliptic _____ is shaped like an oval cup and can have a maximum or minimum point.
    a. Paraboloid
    b. Parametric surface
    c. PDE surfaces
    d. Steiner surfaces

26. With a = b an elliptic paraboloid is a _____: a surface obtained by revolving a parabola around its axis. It is the shape of the parabolic reflectors used in mirrors, antenna dishes, and the like; and is also the shape of the surface of a rotating liquid, a principle used in liquid mirror telescopes. It is also called a circular paraboloid.

a. 1-center problem
b. 11-cell
c. -module
d. Paraboloid of revolution

27. In mathematics, more specifically algebraic topology, a _____ is a continuous surjective function p from a topological space, C, to a topological space, X, such that each point in X has a neighbourhood evenly covered by p. This means that for each point in X, there is associated an ordered pair, (K, U), where U is a neighborhood of x and where K is a collection of disjoint open sets in C, each of which gets mapped homeomorphically, via p, to U (as shown in the image.) In particular, this means that every _____ is necessarily a local homeomorphism.
   a. Cohomology
   b. Topological modular forms
   c. Sheaf cohomology
   d. Covering map

28. _____ is the boundless, three-dimensional extent in which objects and events occur and have relative position and direction. Physical _____ is often conceived in three linear dimensions, although modern physicists usually consider it, with time, to be part of the boundless four-dimensional continuum known as spacetime. In mathematics _____s with different numbers of dimensions and with different underlying structures can be examined.
   a. 1-center problem
   b. -module
   c. 11-cell
   d. Space

29. In topology, two continuous functions from one topological space to another are called _____ if one can be 'continuously deformed' into the other, such a deformation being called a homotopy between the two functions. An outstanding use of homotopy is the definition of homotopy groups and cohomotopy groups, important invariants in algebraic topology.
   a. Homotopic
   b. Spanier-Whitehead duality
   c. 1-center problem
   d. -module

30. A subset of a topological space X is a _____ if it is a connected space when viewed as a subspace of X.

One may perceive mathematical spaces which are not connected. For instance, the space resulting from the deletion of an infinite line from the plane is not connected for two points on opposite sides of the deleted line cannot be joined by a path within the space. Other examples of disconnected spaces (that is, spaces which are not connected) include the plane with an annulus removed, as well as the union of two disjoint disks in two-dimensional Euclidean space.

 a. 1-center problem
 b. -module
 c. Boundary point
 d. Connected Set

31. In topology, a geometrical object or space is called _____ if it is path-connected and every path between two points can be continuously transformed into every other.

Informally, a thick object in our space is _____ if it consists of one piece and does not have any 'holes' that pass all the way through it. For example, neither a doughnut nor a coffee cup (with handle) is _____, but a hollow rubber ball is _____.

 a. 11-cell
 b. 1-center problem
 c. -module
 d. Simply Connected

32. In mathematics, a _____ space is a topological space that admits a basis of simply connected sets. Every _____ space is also locally path-connected and locally connected.
 a. Desarguesian plane
 b. Brocard circle
 c. -module
 d. Locally simply connected

33. In differential geometry, a discipline within mathematics, a _____ is a subset of the tangent bundle of a manifold satisfying certain properties. _____s are used to build up notions of integrability, and specifically of a foliation of a manifold
 a. Banach manifold
 b. Theorema Egregium
 c. G_2-structure
 d. Distribution

Chapter 5. Global Differential Geometry

34. In functional analysis and related areas of mathematics, _____ topological vector spaces or _____ spaces are examples of topological vector spaces (TVS) which generalize normed spaces. They can be defined as topological vector spaces whose topology is generated by translations of balanced, absorbent, convex sets. Alternatively they can be defined as a vector space with a family of seminorms, and a topology can be defined in terms of that family.
   a. 1-center problem
   b. -module
   c. Locally convex
   d. 11-cell

35. In geometry, a polygon can be either _____ or concave.

A _____ polygon is a simple polygon whose interior is a _____ set. The following properties of a simple polygon are all equivalent to convexity:

   • Every internal angle is less than 180 degrees.
   • Every line segment between two vertices remains inside or on the boundary of the polygon.

A simple polygon is strictly _____ if every internal angle is strictly less than 180 degrees. Equivalently, a polygon is strictly _____ if every line segment between two nonadjacent vertices of the polygon is strictly interior to the polygon except at its endpoints.

   a. Separating axis theorem
   b. Convex combination
   c. Supporting hyperplane
   d. Convex

36. In topology, the term degree is applied to continuous maps between manifolds of the same dimension. The _____ can be defined in terms of homology groups or, for smooth maps, in terms of preimages of regular values. It is a generalization of winding number. For example, consider the map z^n on the complex plane. Viewed as a map from S^2 to itself, it has degree n. It wraps the sphere n times around itself.
   a. Degree of a map
   b. 11-cell
   c. -module
   d. 1-center problem

37. In geometry, the terms _____ and polar are used to describe a point and a line that have a unique reciprocal relationship with respect to a given conic section. If the point lies on the conic section, its polar is the tangent line to the conic section at that point.

For a given circle, the operation of reciprocation in a circle corresponds to transforming each point in the plane into its polar line and each line in the plane into its _____.

a. -module
b. 1-center problem
c. 11-cell
d. Pole

38. In topology, the _____ states that every non-self-intersecting loop in the plane divides the plane into an 'inside' and an 'outside' region, and any path connecting a point of one region to a point of the other intersects that loop somewhere. It was proved by Oswald Veblen in 1905.

The precise mathematical statement is as follows.

Let c be a simple closed curve in the plane R^2. Then the complement of the image of c consists of two distinct connected components. One of these components is bounded (the interior) and the other is unbounded (the exterior). The image of c is the boundary of each component.

a. 11-cell
b. Jordan curve theorem
c. -module
d. 1-center problem

39. A _____ is a movement of an object in a circular motion. A two-dimensional object rotates around a center (or point) of _____. A three-dimensional object rotates around a line called an axis.
a. Square lattice
b. Curve of constant width
c. Similarity
d. Rotation

40. In geometry, the _____ line (or simply the _____) to a curve at a given point is the straight line that 'just touches' the curve at that point (in the sense explained more precisely below.) As it passes through the point of tangency, the _____ line is 'going in the same direction' as the curve, and in this sense it is the best straight-line approximation to the curve at that point. The same definition applies to space curves and curves in n-dimensional Euclidean space.

Chapter 5. Global Differential Geometry

a. Tangent
b. Cartan connection
c. Metric signature
d. Measuring function

41. In mathematical study of the differential geometry of curves, the _____ of a plane curve is the integral of curvature along a curve taken with respect to arclength:

The _____ of a closed curve is always an integer multiple of 2>π, called the index of the curve; it is the winding number of the unit tangent about the origin. This relationship between a local invariant, the curvature, and a global topological invariant, the index, is characteristic of results in higher-dimensional Riemannian geometry such as the Gauss-Bonnet theorem.

The _____ of a curve >γ in a higher dimensional Euclidean space (equipped with its arclength parameterization) can be obtained by flattening out the tangent developable to >γ into a plane, and computing the _____ of the resulting curve.

a. Great grand stellated 120-cell
b. Disk covering problem
c. Non-positive curvature
d. Total curvature

42. In mathematics, a _____ of a submanifold of a smooth manifold is an open set around it resembling the normal bundle.

The idea behind a _____ can be explained in a simple example. Consider a smooth curve in the plane without self-intersections.

a. -module
b. 1-center problem
c. 11-cell
d. Tubular neighborhood

43. In mathematics, a _____ is a flat surface. _____ s can arise as subspaces of some higher dimensional space, as with the walls of a room, or they may enjoy an independent existence in their own right, as in the setting of Euclidean geometry

a. Plane
b. Simple polytope
c. Pendent
d. Parallelogram law

44. In mathematics, a _____ is a curve in a Euclidian plane (cf. space curve.) The most frequently studied cases are smooth _____s (including piecewise smooth _____s), and algebraic _____s.
   a. Point group in two dimensions
   b. Heilbronn triangle problem
   c. Chirality
   d. Plane curve

ANSWER KEY

Chapter 1

1. c	2. b	3. d	4. c	5. d	6. a	7. b	8. d	9. d	10. c
11. d	12. d	13. d	14. d	15. a	16. d	17. a	18. b	19. c	20. b
21. d	22. d	23. b	24. a	25. d	26. a	27. d	28. c	29. d	30. d
31. a	32. a	33. d	34. b	35. c	36. b	37. a	38. b	39. b	40. d
41. a	42. c	43. d	44. d	45. d	46. b	47. c	48. c	49. d	50. d
51. b	52. c								

Chapter 2

1. a	2. c	3. d	4. d	5. c	6. d	7. a	8. d	9. d	10. b
11. d	12. c	13. d	14. d	15. d	16. a	17. d	18. b	19. d	20. b
21. b	22. a	23. d	24. d	25. d	26. d	27. d	28. d	29. d	30. d
31. b	32. d	33. a	34. d	35. d	36. d	37. d	38. d	39. c	40. a
41. a	42. b	43. d	44. d	45. c	46. b	47. b	48. b	49. c	50. d
51. b	52. a	53. a	54. a	55. d	56. c	57. d	58. c	59. d	60. a
61. b	62. c	63. d	64. a	65. d	66. a	67. b			

Chapter 3

1. b	2. c	3. b	4. c	5. d	6. c	7. d	8. a	9. d	10. d
11. a	12. b	13. b	14. b	15. d	16. d	17. c	18. d	19. d	20. d
21. c	22. a	23. d	24. d	25. d	26. c	27. b	28. d	29. a	30. a
31. b	32. d	33. c	34. c	35. d	36. b	37. a	38. d	39. d	40. b
41. d	42. c	43. d	44. c	45. d	46. d	47. d	48. c	49. a	50. d
51. b	52. d	53. b	54. d	55. b	56. b	57. b	58. a	59. b	60. a
61. d	62. a	63. d	64. d	65. d					

Chapter 4

1. d	2. d	3. b	4. c	5. d	6. b	7. c	8. d	9. d	10. c
11. a	12. b	13. d	14. d	15. c	16. d	17. c	18. c	19. d	20. d
21. d	22. d	23. d	24. d	25. a	26. d	27. d	28. d	29. c	30. d
31. d	32. d	33. d	34. a	35. b	36. d	37. c	38. a	39. d	40. c
41. d	42. d	43. b	44. a	45. a	46. d	47. b	48. d	49. d	50. d
51. d	52. c	53. d	54. a	55. d	56. a	57. d	58. c	59. c	60. d
61. d	62. d	63. d	64. d	65. a	66. b	67. d	68. d	69. d	70. d
71. b	72. c	73. a	74. a	75. d	76. a	77. c	78. a		

Chapter 5

1. d	2. a	3. d	4. d	5. d	6. b	7. d	8. c	9. d	10. a
11. d	12. d	13. c	14. d	15. d	16. a	17. d	18. b	19. c	20. b
21. a	22. d	23. d	24. d	25. a	26. d	27. d	28. d	29. a	30. d
31. d	32. d	33. d	34. c	35. d	36. a	37. d	38. b	39. d	40. a
41. d	42. d	43. a	44. d						

www.ingramcontent.com/pod-product-compliance
Lightning Source LLC
Chambersburg PA
CBHW081845230426
43669CB00018B/2831